The Reference Guide for Prostate Cancer

I've just finished reviewing your Reference Guide to Prostate Cancer. I've tried to do a thorough job, so you will find comments, changes, and corrections on almost every page. You have provided a wonderful tool for all prostate cancer patients, and I suspect their doctors. I've learned a great deal by going through it. Please let me know how I can get copies once you publish it. You have done a bang-up job on this.

Once you publish, I can see you doing future revisions to keep up with the medical technology. I'd be honored to be an ongoing contributor to your effort.

—Bob Benson
A *very* knowledgeable PC survivor
St. Marys, Ohio

This monograph offers the prostate cancer patient and/or his family a remarkably comprehensive and practical guide covering virtually every issue and aspect of prostate cancer. This book arms the patient with information, together with valuable links to additional information sources; it also provides the insights to tackle the veritable jungle of terms, treatments, options, and vocabulary that can otherwise drown the patient at just the time he needs a lifeline.

Les Winick has created just such a lifeline, and like other patient's guides such as those for breast cancer, this volume should prove of enormous value and be widely successful.

—Steven Evans
Vice President
Genetic Services Management, Inc.

LW Note: Genetic Service Management, Inc. is a company involved in national clinical trials of nutriceuticals for cancer prevention.

When I was first diagnosed with prostate cancer in 1996, I looked for all the information that I could find on this disease and its treatment. It was the Internet, an amazing research tool, that provided me with the most up-to-date information. The patient is on a life or death mission. The websites provided loads of information and the Internet support groups answered my questions.

In March 1998, Taras Wybaczynsky met me and we worked out the possibilities of a mailing list on the Internet for those interested in alternative medicine. Gene Perla, a well-known jazz musician, asked if I wanted to set up a website, and he offered to handle it at no charge.

The site consists of published clinical trials, research papers, articles, plus more than 20 anecdotal testimonials on men using PC-SPES in the treatment of their prostate cancer.

—Mario Menelly
http://www.pc-spes.com

LW Note: Mario sponsors an alternative medicine website, and I asked that he tell us how this came about. *The Reference Guide for Prostate Cancer* contains the addresses of ten Internet discussion groups and 83 Internet websites, all with information relative to prostate cancer.

Prostate cancer, and its many purported cures, requires that we as patients educate, not only ourselves but our doctors. Diagnosed over 2 years ago, and being active in PCa awareness, education and support on an international level, I have seen enough patients make the mistake of placing blind trust in a physician.

If you educate yourself, you'll survive. The best advice I received since my diagnosis of metastatic disease, on Dec. 12, 1997 was: don't do a thing until you get a Ph.D. in PCa. I share that advice whenever I lecture on the subject, men listen, especially those at Square One.

The Reference Guide for Prostate Cancer is the ideal first step at which to start this invaluable process of self-education; a good read, and the perfect tool for the job.

—Taras Wybaczynsky
Ca Survivor and Lecturer

An outstanding publication and a valuable reference tool. The attached document was wonderfully done and a pleasure to proof.

—Monice M. Kaczorowski
Vice-President & Information Specialist
T E S Consultants, Inc.

The Reference Guide for Prostate Cancer relates to every aspect of prostate cancer. It's an invaluable reference for newly diagnosed cancer patients and their families as well as the long-term survivor. Those of us who think we are well-informed about prostate cancer find that there is a vast area of knowledge that we don't have. This book fills in the blank spots and more.

—Paul Anderson
President PC Survivor, and Lecturer
Roots & Sprouts Health Products, Inc.
(708) 784-9143
www.rootsandsprouts.com

The Reference Guide for Prostate Cancer

Acronyms, Abbreviations, Clinical Trials, Drugs, References, Websites, and more

Les Winick
Survivor and Compiler

Health Education Literary Publisher
380 N. Broadway Suite 304
Jerico, NY 11753
Tel: (516) 942-5000 • Fax: (516) 942-5025
E-mail: JL3730@aol.com

 For information, address Health Education Literary Publisher, 380 N. Broadway, Suite 304, Jerico, N.Y 11753

Library of Congress Cataloging in Publication Data

Winick, Lester, 1927-
The reference guide for prostate cancer: acronyms, abbreviations, clinical trials, drugs, references, websites, MultiGraph, and more.
Includes appendices.

ISBN I-883257-08-5
1. Prostate—-Cancer—-Alternative Treatment
2. Herbs—-Drugs—-Clinical Trials
3. Websites

Dedication

To Barbara
my wife,
for her quiet understanding
who silently sat
while I spent hours,
which turned into days,
which turned into weeks,
which turned into months
on the computer and in libraries.

Disclaimer

The Reference Guide for Prostate Cancer was compiled from a search of published sources, medical journals, prostate cancer patient newsletters, the Internet and various books. The information presented here is for reference purposes, and is not intended to replace medical advice or judgment, or in selecting appropriate drugs or treatments.

Any contemplated medical services involving the utilization of the information from this book by the reader should be reviewed and discussed with his personal physician(s), or a respected herbalist, before final decisions are implemented. Terms included are informational, and should not be construed as advocating any specific treatment or protocol by the compiler, nor any support group, university, or pharmaceutical firm.

The compiler, proofreaders, publisher, and others involved in this work neither affirm nor deny the accuracy or suitability of the information contained herein, or assume any liability for the use of this data in evaluation of any drug, supplemental product, clinical trial, Internet information, or any other data contained in this publication.

The absence of typographical errors is not guaranteed. Readers should consult the more complete information available in the package insert of every drug manufacturer, and any distributor information on any nondrug. A full discussion is essential with a physician on any medication, treatment, or other supplement, prior to their use.

Please send notification of any errors, changes, and omissions in *The Reference Guide* to: Les Winick, c/o Health Education Literary Publisher, P.O Box 948, Westbury, N.Y. 11590.

Contents

Foreword

When Les Winick asked me to write the foreword to his compilation of acronyms, abbreviations, drugs and glossary titled *The Reference Guide for Prostate Cancer,* I was somewhat overwhelmed at the diversity and enormity of the information he had assembled.

This is not an ordinary or casual effort. Rather it represents an exceptional degree of perseverance on the part of the compiler, in tackling the vast body of medical information on prostate cancer found in traditional medical literature. Not only that, the equally impressive amount of information available on the Internet seems not to daunt his efforts. And adjunctive to these are the vast fields of folklore and herbal medicine.

The latter has really caught the attention of the compiler. As a prostate cancer survivor himself, he has spared no effort to query his physicians not only on what are the optimal traditional options–medical, surgical, and/or radiation available, but what are the relative efficacies of these options against watchful waiting, and the alternative options of herbal medication.

Considering the likely outcomes, the compiler's research yielded information that the effectiveness of a herbal compound, PC SPES, had been dramatically demonstrated. So this is the therapeutic choice he made after conventional surgical and medical options had been exercised. And while still keeping an open mind on all options, he has become a believer in PC SPES, because, for him, it has indeed worked with remarkable effectiveness.

The efficacy of this herbal preparation has peaked his interest in learning as much as he can on herbal medicine. This is apparent in the considerable space given to such compounds in this *Reference Guide.*

In addition to the emphasis on herbal medicine and products, the guide is a balanced compilation of medical terms–general definitions, to help the reader to understand medical terms which appear in medical and layman's publications; anatomic designations, so that the reader can understand the location and relationship of the various component organs and structures of the genito-urinary system; and descriptive terms, so that the reader can arrive at an understanding of the effects of the adverse changes of prostate cancer and associated non-cancer conditions.

Other sections deal with acronyms and abbreviations, as well as sources of help and information readily available to those with inquiring minds motivated to learn as much as they can about prostate cancer and related effects on the entire body.

This educational tool is a potent coping device, not only for the cancer patient, but for family members who need to know and understand prostate cancer and its effects. We can never truly know what prostate cancer is without patient and persistent inquiry. And it is only as we come to an understanding of the effects of prostate cancer, that the "right" or "best" treatment options can be exercised.

While efforts to effect a cure for prostate cancer continue to engage our best scientific minds, the here and now options available can offer hope and promise of remarkably effective results.

This is what I sense is the objective of the compiler, a prostate cancer survivor himself. It is also my hope that this compilation will lead to an ongoing optimistic outlook to patients and their families who are dealing with prostate cancer.

–*Reuben A. Ramkissoon, MD, FCAP, FASCP*
Anatomic and Clinical Pathologist,
Chairman and Director (retired)
Department of Pathology
and Laboratory Medicine,
Hinsdale Hospital, IL 60521

Dr. Ben Ramkissoon, was born in San Fernando, Trinidad, West Indies. He completed inter arts requirements at Caribbean Union College there, graduating as his class valedictorian in 1950. He proceeded to the United States in 1952 where he pursued the Bachelor of Arts degree in Business Administration and Chemistry, as well as completing the premedical requirements at Pacific Union College. He received his Doctor of Medicine degree from Loma Linda University in 1959, and became a diplomate of the National Board of Medical Examiners in 1960.

His residency and fellowship in anatomic and clinical pathology was successfully completed in 1964 at the Memorial Hospital of Long Beach, affiliated with the University of California, (Irvine). Ben obtained board certification in anatomic and clinical pathology from the American Board of Pathology that year. He is a Fellow of the American Society of Clinical Pathologists, the College of American Pathologists, and the International College of Pathology.

Dr. Ramkissoon has held teaching positions in the Department of Microbiology, Long Beach State College; School of Medical Technology at

Hinsdale Hospital; and was Adjunct Professor of Medical Technology at Andrews University. He has held attending pathology positions at Northwestern University. The array of his professional society affiliations is too long to list here.

After a successful 15-year period of medical practice in Southern California, Ben joined the medical staff at Hinsdale Hospital as an associate pathologist in 1975 and was shortly appointed as the assistant chief pathologist. His appointment as the Chairman of the Department of Pathology and Laboratory Medicine and Laboratory Director followed in 1979. He served in these positions for a decade, supervising a pathologist staff of six members and some 130 technical and support personnel. He is now retired from active medical practice and teaching appointments.

We met many years ago, as we share a joint hobby of collecting stamps and envelopes related to space exploration. When I spent 3 ½ weeks in the hospital, after my radical prostatectomy and subsequent heart attack, Ben found the time to call from California daily to check on my status. When he returned to Hinsdale, he found time to spend part of every day and evening with my family, comforting them.

When I was finally discharged and arrived home from the hospital, Ben and his wife, Connie, brought the traditional medication–chicken soup. It was delicious.

I have the singular privilege of being his Exhibit A–the "live patient" of his practice in clinical pathology! Words alone cannot express my appreciation of this good human being and friend.

–Les Winick

Acknowledegments

Bonnie and Joe Mrowka

I can't fully express my appreciation for the wonderful support and encouragement given by this couple during my hospital stay, immediately after, and every day since. Their understanding and compassion for people is remarkable. They make this a better world.

Joseph Palmieri, M.D.

Much thanks is due to the work of the late Dr. Joseph Palmieri, who published, as far as I can ascertain, the first glossary of prostate cancer terms in 1991.

Special thanks to the staff at Health Education Literary Publishers, Bettye L. Rainwater, Patricia Phelan, and especially James Lewis, Jr. Ph.D, for their confidence in the book. They have made excellent suggestions and helped make the editing process an all-win situation.

Hank Porterfield

Since its founding in February 1990, US TOO has been a primary source of support and education for men diagnosed with prostate disease, in particular prostate cancer. Dr. Joseph Palmiere, an early US TOO member, and prostate cancer survivor, compiled the first listing of terms, and other lists were subsequently put together by additional US TOO leaders.

It is gratifying to see Les Winick take the time and expend the energy to comb all possible sources of terms, names, medications, organizations, and other data. Now when men are studying the peculiarities of their prostate disease, they will have this compendium to fall back on.

US TOO wants to acknowledge the excellent work done by Les Winick, and we trust that prostate cancer patients will find *The Reference Guide for Prostate Cancer* a great help in analyzing the best course of treatment to follow.

—Hank Porterfield
Chairman US TOO, International

Support Groups

When World War II ended, the American Cancer Society began its visitor programs for radical surgery patients to help them cope with the results of cancer treatment. Reach-to-Recovery was initiated in 1952 to help women with the emotional trauma after radical mastectomy surgery. Ostomy clubs were formed in the early 1950s for patients who had a colostomy.

The Cured Cancer Club help individuals handle the stigma of cancer survival in the mid 1950s and cancer support groups began the relationship between cancer and personality. Further studies on the psychological issues faced by patients and families when dealing with the diagnosis of cancer were done in the 1960s. By the 1980s, the sub-specialty of Psychoneuroimmunology (PNI) was established. It deals with the various human processes which impact the cancer experience.

In 1981, Harold H. Benjamin founded the Wellness Community to study the effects of emotions on the cancer experience. Norman Cousins and Bernie Siegel, M.D., publicized the idea of psychosocial support for cancer patients.

US TOO, International was founded in 1990 by a handful of men with prostate cancer so that other men would not have to face this challenge alone. A short ten years later, the organization has established 360 chapters throughout the world with approximately 60,000 members.

Research has shown that cancer patients who join a support group, read and study about their specialized disease, who attempt to reduce stress and negative thinking, live longer and better than those who do not.

Introduction

Lazarus

My first PSA, taken February 1996, read 59.04. The gastroenterologist insisted on this blood test after a routine colonoscopy, taken annually after my colon resection in 1992. I did not know that I had a prostate, nor had I ever given thought about prostate cancer.

Against the advice of my wife, I insisted on getting this cancer out of my body immediately. Surgery was scheduled for March 1996. After the operation, I was told that it had not spread to my lymph nodes and that the operation was successful. If I knew then, what I know now, I would never have had a prostate operation.

Two days later, while preparing to go home the next morning, I had a cardiac arrest while in the hospital. After nine hits with the electric paddles ("eight didn't work," I was told later), I was placed on life support. My wife was told by a cardiologist to notify my children and make arrangements with a funeral home. Now, that's a great bedside manner!

Eight days, and 16 physicians later, (my daughter kept count), various treatments to get my heart beating again failed. A specialist, known as "the electrician" was called in, and finally got the heart beating on its own. I had a triple bypass and was on the road to recovery. "Lazarus" was written on top of my hospital chart.

Four months after my operation, my PSA started a climb from 0.2 reaching 8.6 in July 1998. During this period, I read articles, books, and brochures about prostate cancer. My visit to two chapters of US TOO, International, paid off in a lot of good advice from men exactly the same situation. Some recommended that I try a herbal combination, called *PC SPES*.

A Prostascint examination showed an area which was "suspicious in the bed of resection and in the root of mesentery." The beast had spread. My urologist recommended the "gold standard" of treatment, hormone therapy. I said "NO," and fled. I decided to try *PC SPES* in August 1998. My PSA decreased to 0.1 and has since remained at that level. A follow-up Prostatic Acid Phosphatase test revealed a level of 0.9, which is normal. My cardiologist took me off all medications.

This reference guide was compiled in the hope that men, and their loved ones, can find the answer to any questions about their personal situation, whether they have prostate cancer or benign prostatic hyperplasia.

Hopefully, the physicians' jargon of medical terminology is translated into understandable terms.

Abbreviations of drugs and treatments, as used by physicians and medical reports, are included. Many abbreviations used in this book have more than one meaning. In such instances, the meaning specific to prostate cancer is given.

Under study at the end of a term indicates that the entry is being evaluated by a drug firm, research institution, or private laboratory. References in parenthesis are either names of manufacturers or research institutions.

See **German Commission E** indicates that this herbal watchdog agency has stated that the herb described is either approved, or not approved for its stated use. **University of Texas** indicates that the entry is being reviewed at this institution, Office of Alternative Medicine; it does not indicate approval or disapproval.

Some brand name products and treatments are also included, since many prostate cancer patients refer to these products by their brand name. The search for new medicines and treatments for prostate cancer is rapidly evolving and new scientific terms are constantly being put into use.

Gene therapy and vaccine terms have been included. Many treatments used for other diseases are being modified, and adapted for use on prostate cancer patients.

There are more than one thousand clinical trials, research studies and private tests being conducted. I have tried to select those with the most direct bearing on prostate cancer.

Herbs, minerals, nutrients, and vitamins that have found their way into the treatment of prostate problems are also listed. However, the reader should be aware that while many of these compounds and elements can be beneficial if used correctly, not all are safe or even useful. Just because something comes from nature doesn't mean that it's good for us.

Several appendices are included to make prostate cancer research easier. These include websites, Internet discussion groups, organization abbreviations, and drug firms with their products; how they may be reached by telephone. This information should assist the reader to be an informed patient.

One appendix tells you how to obtain a free personalized MultiGraph of your prostate cancer history. It will give you a different perspective of your disease and treatments.

The motto of one support group, US TOO, is "Learning to Cope through Knowledge and Hope." The Reference Guide is designed to help you gain that knowledge and hope.

I hope that this book will be a valuable reference manual for prostate cancer survivors and their families. Its place in libraries, for the use of laymen and medical personnel, is my desired larger objective.

—Les Winick
March 2000

Male Urogenital Tract

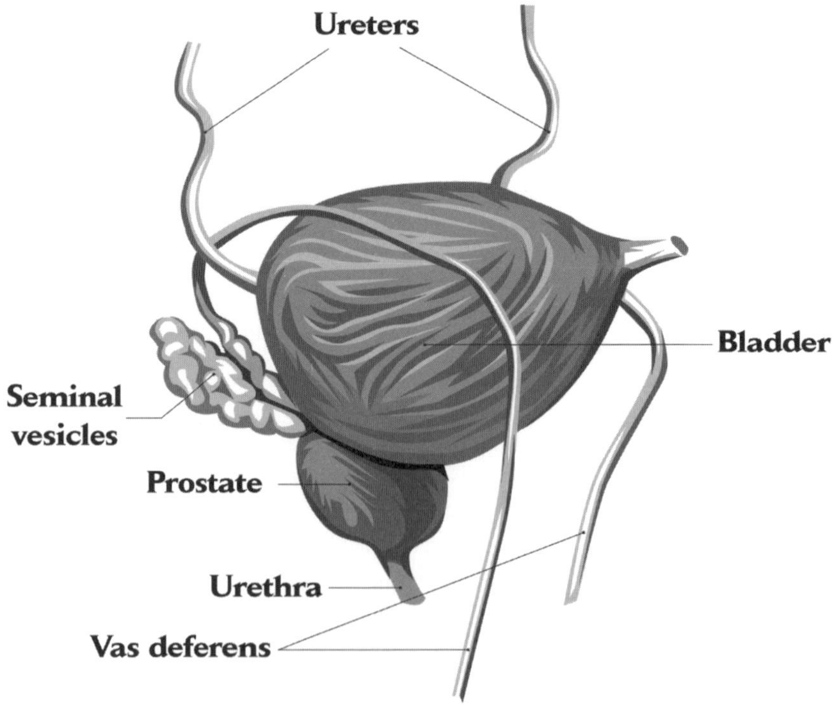

The Reference Guide

2-Methoxyestradiol (2ME2) (EntreMed/NCI): drug that acts as a potent inhibitor of angiogenesis by restricting development of the blood vessels that transport life-sustaining nutrients to tumors; *under study.*

3DCRT 3-dimensional conformal radiation therapy.

3DXRT 3-dimensional external radiation therapy.

5 alpha-dihydrotestosterone male hormone; most active in the prostate.

5-alpha reductose enzyme, found in the prostate, that controls the conversion of testosterone into dihydrotosterone (DHT); useful for stopping growth of a benign prostate tumor.

5 alpha reductase inhibitor drug that prevents the conversion of testosterone to dihydrotestosterone (DHT).

5 AR (5 alpha reductase) enzyme which aids the conversion of testosterone into DHT in the prostate.

5-hete hormone converted from arachidonic acid, high fatty-acid producer, which can encourage cancer cell invasion and new blood vessel formation.

12-hete hormone converted from arachidonic acid, high fatty-acid producer, which can encourage the growth of prostate cancer cells.

15 KD kilodalton (University of Nebraska): serves as an agent to prevent prostate cancer by synthesizing selenium in higher amounts; *under study.*

A

A *see* **aneuploid**.

A, A1, A2 *see* **staging, tumor or cancer**.

AA *see* **adrenal androgens, amino acid, antiandrogen** and **arachidonic acid**.

aaAT antiangiogenic antithrombin; protein that shrinks malignant tumors in mice, apparently by inhibiting the formation of new blood vessels; *under study.*

AAD *see* **adjuvant androgen deprivation**; *also used for* **anemia of androgen deprivation**.

AAH *see* **atypical adenomatous hyperplasia**.

AAT androgen ablation therapy: *see* **ablation, hormonal; androgen**.

AAWR *see* **antiandrogen withdrawal response**.

ab *see* **antibody**.

Abarelix-Depot (Amgen/Praecis): a pure LHRH agonist that suppresses the release of testosterone, a hormone that feeds prostate cancer; *under study.*

abdomen part of the body below the ribs and above the pelvis that contains various organs including the prostate.

abdominal-pelvic CT (computed tomography) X-ray scan used to determine if pelvic lymph nodes have been affected with secondary prostate cancer.

Ablatherm (EDAP TechNomed): treatment system that uses a transrectal high intensity focused ultrasound (HIFU) used for minimally invasive treatment of prostate cancer; this method uses a focused ultrasound beam to destroy well-defined tumors without affecting the surrounding tissue; *under study.*

ablation, hormonal in the management of prostate cancer, the use of various techniques to reduce the level of hormones in the blood to almost zero.

ABP *see* **amino bisphosphonate**.

abscess collection of pus resulting from infection and disintegration of tissue.

absorptiometry diagnostic procedure done on a wrist or spine to determine bone density; a low reading may indicate bone diseases such as osteoporosis.

absorption uptake of a substance into the body or a tissue through the skin or mucous membrane.

absorption coefficient unit of measure used in nuclear medicine; the amount of radiation that is absorbed per unit of thickness, per unit of mass, or per atom of an absorber.

ABT-627 (John Hopkins): endothelial-receptor antagonist that may reduce the pain of metastases as well as lower PSA levels; *under study.*

accessory cell cell that is required in the development of an immune response but does not participate in effector functions.

accuracy ability of test methodology to produce consistent and reproducable results when measured against an acknowledged standard.

acid phosphatase, total, serum (ACP) enzyme that is present in the prostate gland, and in smaller amounts in blood cells, bones, and other body organs; elevated ACP levels may indicate extracapsular prostate cancer and other diseases.

acini parts of a gland in which fluid is produced; singular: acinus.

ACP *see* **acid phosphatase**.

acquired mutations gene changes that arise within individual cells and accumulate throughout a person's lifetime: *also called* **somatic mutations**.

ACTH adrenocorticotrophic hormone produced by the pituitary gland.

Acticon (American Medical Systems): implanted device for fecal incontinence consisting of three components: a cuff around the anal canal, a pressure-regulating balloon, and a pump that the patient operates to open and close the canal to control bowel movements.

Actiq oral transmucosal fentanyl citrate (Anesta/Abbott): a drug used to control pain of prostate cancer; available as a flavored lozenge, which is absorbed by the oral mucosa and enters directly into the bloodstream.

ACTIS fully adjustable penile band for erectile dysfunction.

activated partial thromboplastin time (aPTT) plasma blood test that screens for coagulation, or blood-clotting time.

active hexose correlated compound (AHCC) cyclodextrin (Maypro Industries): made from extracts of several kinds of mushrooms, grown in a liquid medium, and the outer shell of rice bran; an immune system builder.

Actonel risedronate (Hoechst Marion Roussel/Procter & Gamble): drug that may reduce the risk of spinal fractures; may also help to prevent osteoporosis induced by the use of hormone therapy; *under study.*

acupuncture from the Latin for needle (acus) + English (puncture); ancient Chinese art of needle punctures to the body; used for a variety of medical purposes.

ACUS atypical cells of undetermined significance: *see* **atypical cells**.

acute occurring suddenly or within a short period of time.

acute bacterial prostatitis inflammation of the prostate caused by bacteria.

acute-phase proteins serum proteins that are produced rapidly during the initial response to infection or injury.

acute urinary retention inability to urinate, caused by an extended delay in urination, urinary infection, alcohol intake and the use of certain drugs; treated by catherization.

acyclovir (Baylor College of Medicine): gene-injection therapy; *under study.*

Acylfulvenes (Pharmacia & Upjohn): group of novel chemotherapy agents; for hard-to-treat solid tumors; *under study*: *see* **MGI 114**.

AD androgen deprivation: *see* **androgen deprivation therapy**.

adenine purine-base component of the nucleic acids DNA and RNA (determinates of genetic characteristics).

adenocarcinoma cancer that develops from a malignant abnormality in the cell lining or inner surface of an organ such as the prostate.

adenoma benign tumor, with a glandular structure, located within a body part.

adenomatous hyperplasia benign proliferation of any glandular structure in the body; such as in the prostate, colon or uterus.

adenomectomy surgical removal of excess tissue from a gland.

adenopathy enlargement of lymph nodes.

adenoviral-p53 gene (Introgen Therapeutics): synthetic form of the p53 gene; *under study.*

adenovirus group of DNA containing viruses which can be genetically modified and used in gene therapy to treat cancer.

adenovirus transduction action of infecting nondividing cells, which can potentially carry adjunctive quantities of genetic material.

adipose tissue connective tissue that has been specialized to store fat.

adjunctive therapy additional therapy used in the treatment process.

adjustment statistical procedure to account for differences in demographic characteristics among populations that are being compared in a study; often, different age distributions or populations are adjusted so that their influence on outcome variables are more appropriately considered in statistical models.

adjuvant (to a pharmaceutical) any compound that enhances the action of a pharmaceutical; used to define the production of specific antibodies to an antigen.

adjuvant androgen deprivation (AAD) combination of androgen deprivation with other local therapies.

adjuvant therapy additional treatment used to increase the effectiveness of the primary therapy; for example radiation and hormonal adjunctive therapy.

ADR adverse drug reaction.

adrenal androgens (AA) converted to testosterone in the liver, which supplements the supply of testosterone from the testes.

adrenalectomy surgical removal of one or both adrenal glands.

adrenal glands two glands located just above the kidneys that produce a variety of different chemicals.

Adriamycin doxorubicin (Pharmacia & Upjohn): drug used in chemotherapy for refractory prostate cancer.

ADS androgen deprivation syndrome; symptoms that may occur as a result of androgen deprivation therapy.

ADT *see* **androgen deprivation therapy**.

advanced PC cancer that has escaped from the prostate as evidenced by definitive signs, and symptoms, or evidence of locally advanced or metastic disease.

AFGF acidic fibroblast growth compound; protein known to activate endothelial cells: *see* **endothelial cells**.

AG *see* **aminoglutethimide**.

AG 3340 *prinomastat* (Agouron Pharmaceuticals): metalloproteinase (MMP) enzyme inhibitor for hormone-refractory prostate cancer patients; being tested in combination with Novantrone and Prednisone; *under study.*

agar gelatinous material used as a culture medium.

age single most important risk factor for prostate cancer, increasing age is associated with increasing risks.

age-adjusted statistical method used to adjust effects of age of an individual or group of individuals; for example, prostate cancer survival data and average normal PSA values may be adjusted according to the ages of groups of men.

AGM 1470 *see* **TNP 470**.

agonist drug that binds to the same cellular receptors as a natural substance and produces a similar physiological effect; opposite of antagonist.

A/G ratio, serum ratio between total albumin and globulin levels found in the blood.

AHCC *see* **active hexose correlated compound**.

AIPC androgen-independent prostate cancer: *see* **androgen independent cells**.

albumin part of the blood chemistry panel test: principal component of total protein in the plasma; helps regulate the osmotic pressure of the blood; because albumin is synthesized by the liver; this test is done as an aid to evaluate liver function and the nutritive status.

albuminuria presence of albumin in the urine.

alcohol, absolute *ethanol* (John Hopkins) injected into the enlarged prostate gland, in a benign prostatic hyperplasia diagnosis, by dehydrating cells—which causes them to take in water, explode and die*; under study.*

alendronate sodium *see* **Fosamax**.

algorithms mathematical factors used as predictive parameters.

alitretinoin Panretin capsules (Ligand Pharmaceuticals) *under study.*

Alivizatos, Hariton-Tzannis *see* **Greek cancer cure**.

alkaline strongly basic (opposite of acidic) substance; a pH level of more than 7.0 is alkaline, while one with a pH lower than 7.0 is acidic.

alkaline phosphatase an enzyme made by cells in the bone, liver, etc.

alkaline phosphatase, serum (Alk Phos) part of the blood chemistry panel test; an enzyme active in blood plasma or serum; test used to detect metastasis to bones or liver; may be elevated in diseases other than prostate cancer.

alkylating agent chemotherapy drug used in cancer treatment.

allele variant form of the same gene; produces variation in inherited characteristics, such as eye color or blood type.

allogenic vaccine that may include substances common to many cancers in combination with an immune system stimulant such as GM2, a ganglioside molecule: *see* **GM2**.

allogenic transplant tissue used in transplants that has been taken from another person; a transfer of tissue from one person to another: *see* **bone marrow**.

allopathic form of medical practice that treats symptoms.

allopathic medicine conventional medicine as practiced by a graduate of a medical school or college granting an M.D. degree.

allylic sulfides compound containing garlic, onions and scallions; used to promote production of anti-cancer enzymes.

aloe vera *Aloe ferox, a. barbadensis* an extract, carrisyn, may stimulate the immune system; traditionally used for its antibacterial property against a broad range of microbes: *see* **German Commission E**; **University of Texas**.

alopecia hair loss; may be caused in cancer patients by one of the chemotherapeutic drugs or radiation therapy; usually partial and short-term.

alpha-1-adrenergic blockers drugs used to relax symptoms of urinary frequency: *see* **Cardura**, **Hytrin** and **Flomax**.

alpha-blockers pharmaceuticals that act on the prostate by relaxing certain types of muscle tissue; may be used in the treatment of BPH: *see* **benign prostatic hyperplasia**.

Alpha Dry System brand name for a collection condom designed for ease in emptying while in a normal standing position.

alpha-linolenic acid substance found in flaxseed and other fats and oils; may reduce inflammation.

alpha-tocopherol form of vitamin E.

alprostadil vasoactive prostaglandin that occurs naturally in human tissues and fluids, including the semen of fertile men; being tested (NexMed): as a topical cream for erectile dysfunction: *under study*: *see* **Caverject, Edex, Muse, prostaglandin**.

ALT alanine transaminase blood test of an enzyme in the liver; used to diagnose liver diseases, including metastases.

alternative medical system complete system of theory and practice that has been developed outside of the Western biomedical approach.

alternative treatment including homeopathy, holistic medicine, and Chinese medicine; complementary therapy or alternative medicine.

AMAS *see* **anti-malignin antibody in serum**.

Ambrotose (Mannatech): brand name product with unproven claim that it improves the immune system of cancer patients.

amino acid (AA) basic nitrogen-containing substance involved in the making of proteins in all living matter; there are more than 20 amino acids required for normal good health, but the body is only able to make eight essential ones; they are: isoleucine, leucine, lysine, methionine, phenylalanine, threonine, trytophan, and valine. Some of the nonessential amino acids are: alanine, arginine, asparagine, aspartic acid, cysteine, glutamine, glycine, histidine, proline, serine, and tyrosine.

amino bisphosphonate (ABP) may act directly on tumor cells to cause apoptosis: *see* **apoptosis, bisphosphonates**.

aminoglutethimide (AG) used to treat patients with advanced prostate cancer who have failed initial hormone therapy.

amplification an increase in the number of copies of a specific DNA fragment; can occur either in vivo or in vitro.

ampulla dilated end of a duct; a membranous bag or vessel.

AMS 700 (American Medical Systems): inflatable penile prosthesis.

anadron *see* **antiandrogen**.

analgesic pain-relieving medicine such as aspirin, Tylenol, or morphine.

analog synthetic compound similar to the one manufactured by the body; for example, LH-RH analogs Lupron and Zoladex.

Androgel a gel used to treat low testosterone.

anandamide marijuana-like chemical in the brain that works as a natural pain reliever.

Anandron nilutamide (Hoechst Marion Roussel): antiandrogen used to treat metastatic prostate cancer, licensed in Canada: *see* **Nilandron**.

anastomosis location in the body where two different structures are surgically reconnected after a portion has been removed.

anatomical dealing with the physical location and/or structure of organisms.

AND *see* **axillary node dissection**.

Androcur cyproterone acetate (Schering): steroid that blocks androgen receptors at the prostate cell level.

androderm *see* **Surlyn**.

androgen a hormone, (e.g., testosterone), that produces male characteristics and the development and function of male sexual organs; may be used to treat some cancers, but may make some cancers grow; such as prostate cancer. The counterpart for the female sex hormone is estrogen.

androgen ablation elimination of nearly all of the body's supply of male hormones; acts by blocking the effects of remaining androgenic hormones.

androgen blockers medications that prevent hormones from reaching their androgen target cells.

androgen dependent cells prostate cancer cells that depend on hormones to survive.

androgen deprivation therapy (ADT) treatment that reduces testosterone to castration levels; can be accomplished by the use of chemicals: *see* **monotherapy, combined hormonal therapy**.

androgen independent cells prostate cancer cells that do not depend on hormones to reproduce.

androgen receptor (AR) component in the development of the prostate and prostate cancer.

androgen suppressor feature on the cellular surface to which the androgen binds; when taken into the body, it tends to reduce the release of male hormones or their precursors.

andromedin compound that mediates androgen action; refers to the formation, release, utilization, or elimination of such substances or precursors.

androstenedione androgen that is produced naturally in the body by the adrenal cortex, ovary and testes—an adrenal androgen. It has a circadian (a biological timing mechanism) rhythm of secretion with the primary secretion occurring in the morning; a metabolite of DHEA; a testosterone precursor.

androstenedione, serum test to determine the amount of some of the male hormone derivatives of testosterone that are present in the blood.

androsterone sex hormone secreted by the testes and the adrenal glands.

anecdotal may refer to results of a stated treatment carried out without benefit of a clinical trial.

anecdote personal account of an event.

anemia condition characterized by a reduction in the number of red blood cells or in the amount of hemoglobin; concentration in such cells may be treated by blood transfusions.

anergy state caused by an inadequate immune system; absence of reaction to substances that provoke a sensitivity response by the body.

anesthesia medication that causes entire or partial loss of sensation and memory.

anesthetic drug that produces general or local loss of physical sensations, including pain.

aneuploid (ANEUP) having an abnormal number or sets of chromosomes; aneuploid cancer cells tend not to respond well to therapy; may be fast growing: *see* **diploid, tetraploid**.

angelica root *Angelicae radix* herb used to treat mild spasms of the gastrointestinal tract: *see* **German Commission E**.

angiogenesis process of forming new blood vessels, a prerequisite to tumor growth.

angiogenesis inhibitor (Genzyme General): substance that prevents or reduces the growth of new blood vessels to new tissue masses; *under study*.

Angiostatin (EntreMed): drug that fights cancer by blocking the growth of blood vessels needed to feed cancer cells; it is a naturally occurring inhibitor of angiogenesis; *under study*: *see* **Endostatin**.

angiozyme (Ribozyme Pharmaceuticals) a molecule that prevents the VEGF receptor from being formed; under study: *see* **VEGF**.

animal model laboratory animal, usually mice, used in research because of similarities to humans.

ANOVA analysis of variance; statistical technique used to correlate the effect of independent variables, (e.g. diet, age, sex, history), on the outcome of a study being considered.

antagonist drug that binds to a cellular receptor, without producing any physiological effects, thus blocking the binding capacity to any other substance of that receptor; a molecule that specifically counteracts the action of another molecule.

anterior front; the anterior of the prostate is the part of the prostate that faces forward.

antiandrogen (AA) compound, usually a synthetic pharmaceutical, that blocks or otherwise interferes with the normal action of androgen receptor sites in target organ cells.

antiandrogen withdrawal response (AAWR) decrease in PSA caused by the withdrawal of an antiandrogen, such as Bicalutamide or Eulexin, once combined hormonal therapy begins to fail; may occur when sensitized prostate cancer cells that have mutated to feed on antiandrogens; the withdrawal destroys such sensitized cells.

antiangiogenesis therapy use of drugs or other compounds that interfere with the development of new blood vessels that feed the tumor.

antibacterial drug used to treat a prostatic, or other infection, caused by bacteria.

antibiotic compound or pharmaceutical; can kill certain types of bacteria.

antibody protein substance produced by the immune system as a defense against an invading or "foreign" material or substance: *see* **antigen**.

anticholinergic drug that may block the parasympathetic nerves; such as blocking the bladder and genitalia; may be used to treat urinary incontinence, among other conditions.

anticoagulant substance which inhibits blood coagulation.

anti-ED-B-Mab antiangiogenesis drug; *under study*.

antiemetic substance that prevents or relieves nausea and vomiting; used before, during, and after chemotherapy or radiotherapy.

antigen biological substance, such as a vaccine or foreign protein, that produces an immunological response, (e.g., antibodies).

antigenicity capacity of an antigen to elicit an antibody response.

antigonadotropic agent preventing growth or function of the testes or ovary.

anti-inflammatory drug that reduces pain, swelling, etc. resulting from infection or prostatosis.

anti-malignin antibody in serum (AMAS) blood test that can be used for detecting cancer, including prostate; it measures the amount of a malignin polypeptide found in most cancerous cells regardless of their cell type or location; appears to be effective in diagnosing early stage and monitoring treatment of prostate cancer.

antimetabolites anticancer drugs that interfere with the process of DNA production, thus preventing cell division.

antimycotic agent drug that inhibits or destroys fungal infections.

antineoplaston peptides, small amino acid derivatives; work by reprogramming cancer cells to die like normal cells; under review by the FDA: *see* **Burzynski**.

anti-oncogenes tumor suppressor gene: *see* **oncogenes**.

antioxidant substance that inhibits oxidation or reactions; promoted by oxygen or peroxides, and may prevent the deterioration of oils, fats, and other materials; may be useful in treatment of cancer.

antisense a coding sequence of DNA: *see* **TGF-B1**.

antisense phosphorothionate oligonucleotides antiangiogenesis drug; *under study.*

antithrombin III (ATIII) (Genzyme General): protein normally found in human plasma that helps regulate blood clotting; a change in shape, induced by heat or enzymes, may cause the protein to become an angiogenesis, (forming of new blood vessels), inhibitor; *under study.*

Anti-VEGF (Genentech): anti-vascular endothelial growth compound that may attack and destroy the VEGF protein, produced by new tumor blood vessels; *under study*: *see* **VEGF**.

anti-VEGI antiangiogenesis drug; *under study.*

anuria inability to urinate.

anus opening of the rectum where wastes leave the body.

anxiety diffuse, highly unpleasant, often vague feeling of apprehension, accompanied by sensations such as pounding of the heart and sweating; there is an associated anticipation of future misfortune or danger, either external or internal.

Anzemet dolasetron mesylate (Hoechst Marion Roussel): drug used to prevent nausea and vomiting associated with chemotherapy.

A.P. acupuncture physician.

APC adenomatous polyosis cell; precancerous disease: *see* **Aptosyn**.

APC 8015 antigen-presenting cells; for hormone refractory prostate cancer to stimulate immune responses; *under study.*

apex tip or bottom of the prostate; the part of the prostate farthest away from the bladder.

aplidine (Pharma Mar/Zeltia, Spain): substance being developed from sea squirts which may shrink prostate tumors; found in the Mediterranean Sea; *under study.*

apolar containing certain nerve cells; having no radiating process.

Apomate (North American Scientific/Theseus Imaging): imaging technique to show apoptosis, (programmed cell death) in tumors before and after antitumor treatment; may also identify patients whose tumors may not respond to the specific antitumor medicine being used.

apomorphine SL brain chemical involved in sexual response; in lower doses stimulates dopamine; being tested, (TAP Holdings), for erectile dysfunction; *under study.*

apoptosis process by which cells create their own controlled death in response to intracellular or extracellular events; *also called* **programmed cell death**.

APPS alternative therapy in which 900,000 I.U units of vitamin A are applied intramuscularly; the carrier pentosanpolysulfate takes the vitamin into the tumor cell, where it releases lysozymes which destroy the tumor cells.

Aptosyn exisulind (Cell Pathways): lowered PSA levels significantly in trials; has an inhibitory effect upon both the androgen-sensitive LNCap and the androgen-insensitive PC3 prostate cancer cell lines; kills cancer cells while not harming normal cells; when tested in conjunction with other chemotherapies, it works in cancers which are otherwise untreatable; *under study*: *see* **LNCap**.

APTT *see* **activated partial thromboplastin time**.

aquaplast a plastic mold surrounding the pelvis to maintain the correct position for a patient being given radiation treatment.

AR *see* **androgen receptor**.

arachidonic acid amino acid that is a normal constituent of body fluids and present in meat, dairy fat, and egg yolks; considered to be a risk factor for prostate cancer.

Aredia pamidronate (Novartis): drug used to palliate bone pain in advanced prostate cancer.

areola circle of dark-colored skin surrounding the nipple of the breast (male or female).

ARM androgen receptor mutation: *see* **androgen receptor**.

aromatherapy massage with the essential oils of various flowers; the beneficial effects based on the aroma of the ingredients used.

arterial pertaining to an artery or arteries.

artery blood vessel carrying blood away from the heart, walls have smooth muscle, and are innervated by the sympathetic nerves: *see* **sympathetic nerves**.

artificial neural networks (John Hopkins) application of specific computer programs as anaid to doctors and patients to choose optimal prostate cancer treatment; *under study*.

artificial urinary sphincter prosthetic device used to remedy urinary incontinence by constricting the urethra.

art therapy one of the complementary therapies that improve well-being by helping patients express emotions through art thus helping in the healing process.

arylsulfatase A urine test that aids in the diagnosis of cancer of the bladder, rectum, and several other conditions.

ascorbic acid vitamin C.

ascorbic acid tolerance test to determine the extent of vitamin C deficiency, taken after administration of a known amount of ascorbic acid.

asparaginase *see* **Elspar**.

asparagus root *Asparagi rhizoma* herb traditionally used for infections of the urinary tract: *see* **German Commission E**.

aspartate aminotransferase, serum (AST) liver function test; usually done as part of a liver or biochemical profile; a method to assess damage or inflammation of the liver that may be caused by medication, such as chemotherapy agents: *also known as* **SGOT**.

aspartic acid one of the nonessential amino acids present in body fluids; may decrease fertility in men through decreased sperm count or sperm mobility.

aspiration biopsy use of suction to remove fluid or cells from the body; usually through a fine needle.

aspirin white analgesic/anti-inflammatory crystalline powder primarily for reducing fever, and relieving pain.

assay determination of the amount, purity, or potency of a substance; a PSA test is sometimes called a *PSA assay*.

AST *see* **aspartate aminotransferase, serum**.

astragalus *Astragalus membranaceous* herb that may have immune-enhancing properties.

asymptomatic without obvious signs or symptoms of disease; when prostate cancer is in its early stages, it may develop and grow without producing any symptoms.

ATBC alpha-tocopherol, beta-carotene cancer prevention study.

AT III *see* **antithrombin III**.

ATF amino terminal fragment, a highly active part of a uPA molecule: *see* **uPA**.

atomic tests study found higher death rates of leukemia, nasal and prostate cancer, among soldiers who took part in atomic tests.

ATP adenosine-triphosphate test, also called the *CK assay* test.

ATRA all-trans-retinoic acid, a naturally occurring derivative of vitamin A.

Atragen atrageno (New York Presbyterian Hospital/Aronex): drug involving retinoids and interferon alpha being tested for the prevention and treatment of prostate cancer; may have an effect on epidermal growth compound; *under study*: *see* **retinoic acids**.

atrophy a wasting away or diminution in the size of cell, tissue, organ or limb.

atypia histological or cytological abnormal changes in tissue (cells): *see* **dysplasia, PIN**.

atypical not usual, abnormal.

atypical adenomatous hyperplasia (AAH) glandular structures such as the prostate that have begun to show abnormal changes, compared to the expected normal features; early manifestation of cellular changes which may eventually develop into cancer.

atypical cells not usual; abnormal precursors to abnormal cells which may become malignant.

AUS artificial urinary sphincter.

autochthonous found in the place of formation; not removed to a new site.

autocrine secretion of a substance, such as a growth compound, that stimulates the activity of the secretory cell itself.

autoimmune disease immune response directed against one's own body tissues.

autoimmunity condition in which the body produces an immune response against its own tissue constituents.

autologous donation of blood donation of ones own blood for a transfusion, in case the need arises during or after a medical procedure.

autologous transplant donor tissue used in a transplant is obtained from the recipient; may be used immediately at another site, such as a skin transplant, or may be stored and used later, such as in a bone marrow transplant.

autologous vaccine preparation used to treat the patient's condition; obtained from a process of combining the patient's own cancer cells with an agent that results in a significant immune response.

autoradiography technique that uses X-ray film to visualize radioactively labeled molecules, or fragments of molecules; may be used to analyze the length and number of DNA fragments after they are separated by gel electrophoresis.

autosomal dominant pattern of inheritance in which one parent with a genetic expression has a 50 percent chance of passing it on to a child; may be familial diseases or conditions.

autosome any ordinary paired chromosome, as distinguished from a sex chromosome; human cells contain 22 pairs of autosomes.

axilla armpit.

axillary node dissection (AND) examination of the lymph nodes from the underarm (axilla) that have been removed during surgery in order to assess the spread of cancer; the number of nodes in this area varies.

B

B0-B2 *see* **staging, tumor or cancer**.

B-0829 antiangiogenesis drug; *under study.*

bacteria microscopic one-celled plants that may cause prostate or other infections.

bacterial prostatitis *see* **prostatitis**.

bacteriophage cell that destroys bacteria.

baicalein saponin, extracted from the root of Scutellaria; *sometimes known as* **Skullcap**; in a Chinese herb, that may inhibit cancer cell multiplication.

balloon dilation small, inflated balloon inserted through a catheter into the part of the urethra that runs through the prostate; the urethra is stretched permitting urine to flow more easily; the balloon is then deflated and removed.

barberry *Berberis vulgaris* used for ailments of the urinary tract: *see* **German Commission E, Not approved**.

barley green juice extract of young barley plant; some claim it has a beneficial effect on prostate cancer.

base wide part of the top of the prostate closest to the bladder.

baseline initial value, (e.g., PSA), that is taken prior to starting or changing treatment; the baseline value is used for comparison with future values to assess the effectiveness of the treatment.

baseline bone mineral density *see* **bone mineral density**.

base pair two bases, such as adenine and thymine or guanine and cytosine, that are bonded together.

basophil white blood cell that combats parasitic infections.

BAT product that combines an ultrasound probe, and a 3D tracking system, with a treatment- room interface to pinpoint target organs at the time of radiation treatment; reduces the need for targeting margins, which have been used to compensate for errors in the localization of tumors.

Batimastat antiangiogenesis drug; replaced by Marimastat.

BAY 12-9566 antiangiogenesis drug in clinical trials; *under study*.

BB 2516 *see* **Marimastat**.

B-cells class of white blood cells originating in the bone marrow and found in blood, spleen, and lymph nodes; precursors of plasma cells that secrete antibodies directed against invading antigens: *also known as* **B-lymphocytes**.

BCL2 a suppressor of apoptotic cell death: *see* **apoptosis**.

BCL6 gene that enhances immune function.

bee pollen *Apis mellifica* pollen of a bee, traditionally used to help reduce prostate problems by helping to inhibit prostate growth.

benign relatively harmless; not cancerous; not malignant.

benign prostatic hyperplasia (BPH) noncancerous condition of the prostate in which the prostate grows, and pushes against the urethra and the bladder, blocking the flow of urine; there is an abnormal multiplication of the nonmalignant prostate cells.

Stage 1 is marked by urination frequency, delayed urination, and a weak urinary stream. Stage 2 is marked by the start of the decline of the bladder function, resulting in residual urine in the bladder, and the urge to urinate. Note: a man can have BPH and prostate cancer at the same time.

benign prostatic hypertrophy similar to benign prostatic hyperplasia, but caused by an increase in the size of cells rather than the growth of more cells.

benign tumor noncancerous growth that does not spread to other areas of the body.

beta-carotene naturally orange pigment found in yellow and dark green fruit and vegetables such as apricots, squash, cantaloupe, broccoli, spinach, sweet potatoes, and notably carrots; during a study of its cancer-fighting ability, it was found to be effective, when used with aspirin, in the prevention of heart attacks.

beta glucan compound extracted from yeast cell walls; possibly a safe immune stimulant; has been shown to relieve the signs and symptoms of prostate cancer.

beta-lapachone (Dana Farber Cancer Institute): from the red or purple lapacho plant; when used in conjunction with Taxol, may kill cancer cells in laboratory experiments; *under study*: *see* **Pau D'Arco**.

beta-sitosterol key element in saw palmetto, a common palm; may bind to cholesterol to reduce its absorption.

bFGF basic fibroblast growth compound; a protein known to activate the endothelial cell: *see* **endothelial cells** and **VEGF**.

bias in research any systematic error in procedures, results, or inferences that deviate from the "truth"; deviations can occur because of design flaws in a study design, such as data collection, or analysis methods.

Bicalutamide *also known as* **Casodex**.

bid *(Latin: bis in die)*: twice each day, may mean about every twelve hours.

bilateral both sides, a bilateral orchiectomy is one in which both testicles are removed.

bilateral extracapsular extension prostate cancer that has grown through both lobes of the prostate: *also known as* **locally advanced prostate cancer**.

bilirubin panel, serum (Bili) part of the blood chemistry panel test; measures the amount of bile pigment that normally circulates in the plasma and is taken up by liver cells.

bilirubinuria presence of bilirubin, a pigment of bile, in the urine.

binomial nomenclature two-part scientific name assigned to all living organisms; the first term is known as the genus (related group), and the second refers to the specific epithet (a given species).

bioassay quantitative determination of the potency of a substance through the measurement of its effects on tissues, living experimental animals, or humans.

biochemical flare *see* **flare reaction**.

bioelectrical therapy (American Biologics, Mexico): claims that this procedure of using electricity changes cancer cell polarity.

bioelectromagnetics unconventional use of electromagnetic fields for medical purposes.

biofeedback process of learning how to control inner functions of the body through mind control and electronic survey; may be used to manage pain.

biofield medicine systems that use subtle energy fields in and around the body for medical purposes.

bioflavonoid term for biologically active flavonoids: *see* **flavonoids**.

bioimpedance (John Hopkins) using an electrical property of cells to improve the prostate biopsy; *under study*.

biological therapy form of cancer treatment based on the knowledge of molecular biology, immunology, and genetics.

biomarker cellular or molecular indicator of exposure, health effects, or susceptibility.

biomodulation theory using nutrients, botanical, or synthetic agents, in order to exploit tumor biology for therapeutic advantage; hopefully to block prostate cancer progression by such interventions.

biopsy (Bx) removal of a sample of tissue in order to check if cancer is present; biopsies are usually carried out under ultrasound guidance, using a spring loaded biopsy gun with which a large hollow needle removes a core or plug of the tissue; a fine needle biopsy is used to aspirate the tissue from a suspected tumor site. It is recommended to wait at least one week after a biopsy before drawing blood for a PSA.

biotechnology science of manipulating life forms to provide desirable products.

biotherapy treatment used to stimulate the body's immune system; based on the knowledge of molecular biology, immunology, and genetics.

biotin essential nutrient required for cell growth and the production of fatty acids; experimentation is being conducted on other uses: *also known as* **vitamin B-6, B-7**.

Bipolar urological loop (ArthroCare): device used for resection of prostate tissue and nonmalignant tumors of the bladder wall.

birch leaf *Betulae folium* herb traditionally used for flushing out infections of the urinary tract: *see* **German Commission E**.

Biosafe PSA4 in-home blood collection kit used as a test for PSA.

bisphosphonates drugs that inhibit bone-turnover by decreasing the resorption of bone; includes alendronate, clodronate, etidronate, and pamidronate.

black tea amber colored beverage; named black tea, because of the color of the leaves.

bladder hollow organ in which urine is collected and stored in the body; one end is connected to the ureters, which brings the urine from the kidneys; the other end is connected to the urethra, which carries the urine out of the body through the penis.

bladder cancer test (Cambridge University, England): urine test; detects a protein given off in large amounts from cancer cells present in the urine; may diagnose bladder cancer in its early stages, could be adapted to test for colon, prostate and other cancers; *under study*.

bladder catheterization passage of a catheter tube into the urinary bladder through the urethra.

bladder neck portion of the bladder that opens into the urethra and permits control of the urine; the input from the brain either relaxes the muscles in the neck of the bladder so that urine can flow, or tightens them so that urine remains in the bladder.

bladder neck contracture surgical complication following prostatectomy causing scarring of the bladder neck; may cause future urinary problems requiring surgical repair.

bladder neck warmer protects the bladder neck from the freezing process of cryosurgery.

bladder outflow obstruction condition may be caused by locally advanced prostate cancer; usually an indication of benign prostatic hyperplasia.

bladder stones a condition where small stones form within the urinary tract.

blastic lesions increased density of bone; seen on X-rays, may be caused by prostate cancer secondary bone tumors, or metastases.

blind study research study in which the subject(s) and/or observer(s) are not told which experimental group the subjects are assigned to; when the subjects and observers are not informed, the study is considered double blind: *see* **double blind study**.

blood chemistry panel (Chem 25) analysis of multiple components of the blood serum, usually includes tests to evaluate function of the liver and kidneys, levels of minerals and cholesterol, etc.; abnormal values can indicate spread of cancer or side effects of treatment: *see* **chem-screen panel**.

blood count enumeration number of white blood cells (which protect against infection), red blood cells (which transport oxygen), and platelets (necessary for blood clotting).

blood tests samples of a patient's blood utilized for testing of various diseases; may be used to evaluate various functions of the body.

blood urea nitrogen (BUN) part of the blood-chemistry panel test; a waste product of protein metabolism produced by the liver and excreted by the kidneys; high values usually mean kidney failure; (e.g., inability of the kidney to remove BUN).

B-lymphocytes *see* **B-cells**.

BMD *see* **bone mineral density**.

BMS-217380 *tesmififene hydrochloride* (Bristol Myers Squibb) *under study.*

BMT *see* **bone marrow transplant**.

bone marrow soft, fatty tissue that fills the cavities of bones and is the birthplace of the cells that circulate in the blood; chemotherapy depresses the bone marrow, resulting in a temporary decrease in the number of the body's circulating blood cells, which are normally manufactured in the bone marrow: *see* **allogenic transplant**.

bone marrow transplant (BMT) transplantation of bone marrow from a healthy donor to a patient under treatment, to stimulate production of formed blood cells.

bone mineral density (BMD) evaluation of bone density.

bone pain pain often due to pressure and local invasion of nerve endings caused by the spread of prostate cancer.

bone scan (BS) more sensitive technique than conventional X-rays; utilizing a radioactive agent injected into the bloodstream to identify abnormal or cancerous growths within or attached to bone. In the case of prostate cancer, a bone scan is used to identify metastases of cancer cells that have escaped from the prostate and set up house in a bony location; metastases appear as "hot spots" on the film; however, the absence of hot spots does not prove the absence of tiny locations of microscopic metastases; suspicious areas are often difficult to distinguish from arthritis.

borage oil *Borago* flowering plant with edible blossoms; contains a high quantity (26%) of the essential fatty acid, gamma linolenic: *see* **German Commission E, Not approved**.

boswellia serrata *Bosewellia carteri* herb traditionally used for urinary-tract infections.

bovine cartilage type of tissue derived from cow sources; claims made as a strong antiangiogenic property.

bovine growth hormone (BGH) genetically engineered drug given to dairy cows; indirect evidence suggests that BGH might contribute to prostate and breast cancer in humans.

bowel, J preparation cleaning of the bowel or intestines prior to abdominal surgery such as radical prostatectomy.

BP blood pressure.

BPH *see* **benign prostatic hyperplasia; prostatitis**.

BPSA baseline PSA taken prior to diagnosis.

brachytherapy (Brachy, BT) form of radiation therapy in which radioactive seeds or pellets, (which emit radiation), are implanted into the gland in order to kill cancerous tissue, (e.g., the prostate, including prostate cancer cells); these seeds may be temporarily or permanently implanted: *also known as* **seed pods**.

bRFS biochemical relapse-free survival.

BRM bone resorption marker.

BS *see* **bone scan**.

BT see **brachytherapy**.

buchu leaf *Barosmae folium* flower leaf used for treatment of inflammation and infection of the kidneys and urinary tract: *see* **German Commission E, Not approved**.

bulbous urethra enlarged section of the urethra where semen fluids collect prior to ejaculation.

BUN *see* **blood urea nitrogen**.

burning bush *Dictamnus albus* herb traditionally used for digestive disorders and diseases of the urinary tract.

Burton, Lawrence, Ph.D. a zoologist, Burton developed a theory during the 1950s that cancer cells multiply when four factors of the immune system fail to recognize and destroy them; results of his experiments as reported in a 1961 article in *Science* could not be replicated. Burton established the Immunology Research Foundation in 1973 in Great Neck, NY; the clinic closed in 1977 and was later reopened as the Immunology Researching Centre Ltd. in Freeport, Grand Bahamas. It was again closed in 1985 and allowed to reopen in 1986; claims that more than 5,000 patients have received immune augmentation therapy in Freeport; *see* **Govallo, Valentin I, M.D.**

Burzynki, Stanislaw R. developer of an antineoplaston therapy which is claimed to cause cancer cells to undergo differentiation, and eventually cause them to die through programmed cell death; supposed to parallel the human immune system.

Buserelin *see* **Suprefact**.

Bx *see* **biopsy**.

C

C225 (ImClone Systems/Merck): monoclonal antibody that targets and inhibits cancerous cells through induction of a natural process of cell death; *under study.*

C,C1,C2 *see* **staging, tumor or cancer**.

Ca carcinoma or cancer; also symbol for calcium.

CA chemotherapy treatment consisting of Cytoxan, in addition to Adriamycin.

CAB *see* **combined androgen blockade**.

cabbage extracts extract of cabbage possessing very strong anticancer properties; researchers are attempting to discover the composition of the active molecules within the extract.

cabergoline *see* **Dostinex**.

cachexia state of ill health, malnutrition, and wasting away of the body that may occur during chronic disease.

CAI carboxyamidotriazole antiangiogenesis drug undergoing clinical trials; *under study.*

calcitonin-salmon *see* **Miacalcin**.

calcitriol *see* **Rocaltrol**.

calcium, serum part of the blood chemistry panel test: calcium is elevated because of changes in the metabolism of bone due to metastatic disease, thus resulting in high calcium levels; a normal blood calcium level is essential for normal function of the heart, nerves, and muscles, and the blood-clotting process.

calculi *see* **bladder stones**.

calmodulin a cancer-binding protein.

CAM complementary/alternative medicine.

CanCell alternative therapy, originally called Entelev, which is a liquid that was claimed to cure cancer by lowering the voltage of the cell structure by about 20 percent; supposedly caused the cancer cells to be digested by, and replaced with normal cells: promoters claim that the liquid can not be analyzed because it varies with vibrations in the atmosphere and keeps changing its energy.

cancer growth of abnormal cells in an uncontrolled manner in the body; unlike benign tumors, cancer cells invade surrounding tissues, and spread to distant sites of the body via the blood stream and lymphatic system.

candidate gene gene whose protein product indicates that it could be the suspect disease gene.

canstatin (Beth Israel Deaconess Medical Center): anti-angiogenisis agent that inhibits new blood vessel growth, suppresses prostate, renal tumor growth in mice; *under study*.

CaP cancer of the prostate.

CAPB cancer of the prostate and brain; a gene associated with a type of prostate cancer; shows a family pattern of occurrence.

capsaicin *Cayenne, Capsicum species* natural decongestant that may contain cancer-fighting properties; found in hot peppers: *see* **German Commission E**.

capsule fibrous tissue that acts as a covering or an outer lining of the prostate; if cancer penetrates this covering, it is no longer considered to be localized.

carboplatin chemotherapy agent used in treatment of a variety of common cancers, including bladder cancer.

Carboxyamidotriazole antiangiogenesis drug in clinical trials; under study.

carcino embrionic antigen (CEA) tumor marker which is also expressed by prostate and other cancers; an elevated CEA has been found in 30 percent of newly diagnosed prostate cancers prior to the PSA test.

carcinogen cancer-causing agent.

carcinoma form of cancer that originates from epithelial cells; cells lining the external or comprising the internal surfaces of some of the organs of the body; carcinomas may also spread to distant sites, such as the lung, liver, lymph nodes, and bone: *see* **metastasis**.

carcinoma in situ cancer that is still confined to the cells of origin and has not invaded the surrounding tissue, or spread outside the area; this stage of cancer is highly curable.

carcinosarcoma rare prostate tumor, made up of both epithelial and connective tissue; usually has a poor prognosis.

Cardura doxazosin (Pfizer): alpha blocker used to treat benign prostatic hyperplasia: *see* **alpha-1-adrenergic blockers**.

carnivora *Dionaea muscipula* plant extract; a phytopharmaceutical that claims to attack and destroy all varieties of cancer; claimed to be especially effective on primitive tumor tissues; blocks the protein kinases in the tumor cell, and deprives it from its necessary proteins; immune-stimulating.

carotenoids pigment found in plants and animals; may reduce the ability of carcinogen-treated cells to transform into malignant cells; sources are vitamin A precursors; yellow, orange, and dark greens.

Cartilade LED brand name for a shark cartilage extract delivered through liposomes; claims that it is fully absorbed by the body: *see* **liposomes**.

Casodex calutamide (Zeneca/Astra): nonsteroidal antiandrogen used to treat advanced prostate cancer.

caspases enzymes that may be the effector of programmed cell death; attack proteins.

castration effective removal (medical or surgical) of the testes (male) and ovaries (female): *see* **orchiectomy.**

CAT *see* **computerized axial tomography**.

catheter hollow (usually flexible plastic) tube that can be used to drain fluids from, or inject fluids into the body; prostate cancer patients have a transurethral catheter drain urine for some time after treatment by surgery, or radiation therapy.

catheterization (urethral) insertion of a catheter via the urethra.

catheterized urine specimen collection of urine through a catheter under sterile conditions.

Cat scan (CT scan) method of combining images from multiple X-rays under the control of a computer to produce cross-sectional, or three-dimensional pictures of the internal organs, which can be used to identify abnormalities; can identify prostate enlargement, but is not always effective for assessing the stage of prostate cancer; significantly more accurate for evaluating metastases to lymph nodes or distant soft tissue sites.

cat's claw *Una del gato* herb grown in the Amazon area; may reduce the side effects of chemotherapy, reduce inflammation, and boost the immune system. Rene Caisse, R.N., used it for 50 years to treat terminally ill cancer patients; she stated that hard-tissue herbs must be boiled, whereas soft-tissue herbs must be simmered below a certain temperature, or they are ineffective: *see* **German Commission E, Not approved**; **University of Texas**.

cavax malignin (General Cancer Vaccine): first synthetic human general vaccine; an antimalginin antibody; *under study.*

caveolin (Baylor College of Medicine) protein being studied as a marker of prostate cancer metastasis; *under study.*

Caverject alprostadil (Pharmacia & Upjohn): drug used to treat erectile dysfunction, self-injected directly into the penis, it produces an erection by relaxing the trabecular smooth muscle and by dilating the cavernosal arteries, localized in the penis.

CaverMap (UroMed): surgical aid that uses a live electric probe to locate the pelvic nerves prior to dissection; can be used to locate and test the cavernous nerve; may be used in a radical prostatectomy with or without a nerve graft.

cavernous body chambers of spongy tissue that make up the shaft of the penis that fills with blood to effect erection.

cavernous nerves tiny nerves that nestle on either side of the prostate gland; vital for erectile function.

CBC *see* **complete blood count**.

CCDRT cell culture drug resistance testing; experimental testing method that determines how mutations create drug resistance in patients.

CDKI *see* **cyclin-dependent kinase inhibitor**.

CDUS *see* **color-flow doppler ultrasound**.

CEA *see* **carcinoembryonic antigen**.

Celebrex celecoxib (Searle/Pfizer): nonsteroidal, anti-inflammatory painkiller used to alleviate pain in the joints.

celecoxib *see* **Celebrex**.

Celera Genomics firm mapping genes via computer decoding.

cell fundamental structural and functional unit of life; the living tissue of every multicelled organism is composed of these fundamental living units and their products.

cell culture process of growing cells in a nutrient solution or material outside the body.

cell cycle pattern of cell division; some cell types divide at a greater frequency than others.

cell differentiation process whereby descendants of a common parental cell achieve and maintain specialization of structure and function.

cell portal *see* **receptor**.

cell saver blood blood recovered during an operation that is transfused back into the patient.

cell specific cancer therapy (CSCT) alternative therapy exposes the patient to a magnetic field to "destroy active cancerous cells in a body and to do so without causing any damage to healthy cells." It is claimed that cancerous cells have an "atypical metabolic mechanism that makes them susceptible to polarizing electromagnetic fields."

cell surface receptors protein structures on the surface of cells that tightly bind specific molecules; a functional part of information transmission to the cell.

cellular immune response immune response that is carried out by specialized cells, in contrast to response carried out by soluble antibodies: *also known as* **cell-mediated immunity**.

central zone area of the prostate gland that makes up about 25 percent of the normal prostatic volume.

c-erbB-2 oncogene that codes for a protein similar to the epidermal growth compound receptor: *see* **oncogene**.

cesium chloride (ScCl) caustic salt that is supposed to alkalize blood slightly causing tumor-cell death; used in combination with concentrated aloe vera.

CgA *see* **chromogranin A**.

CGAP cancer genome anatomy project establishment of an index platform of all genes that are expressed in tumors; the tumor type with the highest representation in the CGAP is prostate cancer.

Chamomile *Matricaria recutita* herb used to treat inflammation of the gastrointestinal tract: *see* **German Commission E**.

CHB combined hormone blockade.

CHBNDT combined hormone blockade non-detectable (PSA) time.

chelation term for removal of ionic elements from the blood: *see* **chelation therapy**.

chelation therapy treatment may involve the intravenous injection of a prescription drug, ethylenediaminetetra acetic acid, which is approved by the FDA for ridding the human body of excess heavy metals; claims that it has been effective in treating atherosclerosis were declared false and misleading on Dec. 18, 1998, by the Federal Trade Commission.

chemiluminescent assays (Quest Diagnostics/Diagnostic Products): test to detect extremely minute amounts of PSA that may be secreted by tissue cells other than prostate cancer cells.

chemo: *see* **chemotherapy**.

chemoprevention use of a pharmaceutical or other substance to prevent the development of cancer.

chemotherapy (Chemo) use of pharmaceuticals or other chemicals to kill cancer cells; in many cases, chemotherapeutic agents kill not only cancer cells but also other cells in the body, which makes such agents potentially very dangerous; may be taken by mouth, or put into the body by needle into a vein, artery, or muscle; considered a systemic treatment because as the drugs travel through the body, they can kill cancer cells anywhere in the body.

chem-screen panel comprised of A/G ratio, albumin, alkaline phosphatase, ALT (SGPT), AST (SGOT), bilirubin, BUN/creatinine (calculated), calcium, carbon dioxide, chloride, cholesterol, creatinine, gamma glutamyltransferase, globulin (calculated), glucose, iron, lactate dehydrogenase, phosphate (as phosphorus), potassium, protein (total), sodium, triglycerides, urea nitrogen (BUN), and uric acid: *see* **blood-chemistry panel (Chem 25)**.

Chiroscience/Darwin (Bristol-Meyers Squibb): firm investigating the genetic field.

chlamydia sexually transmitted bacterial infection that may cause pain during urination.

chlorella fresh water single-celled plant rich in proteins, vitamins, and minerals; may improve resistance to abdominal tumors.

chloride part of the blood-chemistry panel test: an ion controlled by the kidneys and adrenal glands; important in biologic cell function.

cholesterol (chol) part of the blood-chemistry panel test: used to make essential body substances such as cell walls and hormones; high levels are associated with heart disease; some fractions are more desirable in the preservation of good cardiovascular function.

cholesterol/HDL ratio ratio of total cholesterol to HDL cholesterol, a predictor of cardiovascular disease; the lower the ratio, the better the patient outlook.

choline biological source of methyl groups.

chondroitin coating on prostate cancer cells that prevents the immune system from attacking the cancer cells.

chromatin portion of a cell's nucleus that can be stained.

chromogranin A (CgA) test on tissue that may be used to detect prostatic cancer in patients whose PSA is not elevated; small cell tumors grow faster; may involve liver, lung, and lymph nodes in unusual sites.

chromosomes structures found in the nucleus of a cell, which contains the genes, the basic units of heredity; comes in pairs, a normal human cell contains 46: 22 pairs of autosomes, (paired chromosomes), and 2 sex (X/Y) chromosomes; the Y chromosome distinguishes the male inheritance pattern. The National Center for Biotechnology Information reports that the 46 chromosomes house 3,000 million base pairs of DNA and encode about 60,000 to 80,000 proteins; these coding regions make up only about 2 percent of the genome; the function of the remaining 98 percent is unknown.

chromosome translocation exchange of genes, or portions of gene, between different chromosomes.

chromatin-negative lacking sex chromatin and characteristic of the cells of females (XX).

chromatin-positive containing sex chromatin and characteristic of the cells of males (XY).

chronic bacterial prostatitis inflammation of the prostate caused by bacteria.

chronic illness illness extending over a long period of time.

chronic prostatitis *see* **prostatitis**.

chrysin *Passiflora corerulea* male body builders use it to enhance the production of testosterone and to suppress the effect of estrogen on their breasts.

CHT *see* **combined hormonal therapy**.

CHT 2 combined hormonal therapy; the simultaneous use of two drugs, (e.g., Lupron and Casodex), to interfere with the production of testosterone.

CHT 3 combined hormonal therapy; the simultaneous use of three drugs, for example; Lupron, Casodex, Eulexin or Zoladex, plus Proscar; to interfere with the production of testosterone.

CI 994 antiangiogenesis drug; ***under study***.

CLAL cancer, longevity, ancestry and lifestyle study (Yeshiva University): study of Jewish men looking at environmental and genetic factors that may be associated with prostate cancer.

class prediction process to classify active genes to determine cancer.

CLE ***see*** **complete local excision.**

Climara estradiol transdermal (Berlex): patch applied to the skin and releases estrogen into the body; used for the prevention of osteoporosis, as well as to treat other conditions.

clinical flare *see* **flare reaction**.

clinical trial carefully planned experiment to evaluate a treatment or a medication, (often a new pharmaceutical), for an unproven use: *see* **Phase I, II, III,** and **IV**.

clodronate *see* **bisphosphonates**.

clone reproduction of a cell in its exact image.

cloning vector DNA molecule that originates from a virus, plasmid, or cell of a higher organism into which another DNA fragment of another size can be integrated without loss of vector capacity for self-replication.

clonogenicity ability of malignant cells to develop colonies.

CM 101 antiangiogenesis drug; *under study*.

CMA-676 (Wyeth-Ayerst): lab-created antibody intended to target a marker on cancer cells; *under study*.

CN706 (Calydon): utilizes the PSA gene, the DNA region, and is responsible for the specificity of the PSA test; a new virus that would selectively replicate in, and kill prostate cancer cells; *under study.*

CNS central nervous system.

coagulase enzyme that speeds the blood clotting process.

coagulation (coag) process of clotting of blood.

codon refers to the position of a DNA 3-base coding message in the gene sequence.

Coenzyme Q-10 *Upiquinone* member of a class of compounds known as quinones; nonvitamin nutrient said to act as an antioxidant that brings extra energy to the cells of the immune system; mechanism of its anticancer property is currently not well understood, but in several reported patient studies with various metastasized cancers, (some considered terminal), showed improvement: *see* **University of Texas**.

Coenzymes lipid- soluble vitamin that activates acids by forming esters.

COL-3 antiangiogenesis drug in clinical trials; *under study.*

Coley toxin biological therapy that has existed since 1890 and is being investigated again utilizing a method designed to find the tumor, focus the immune system, producing lymphokine to attack the cancer: *see* **University of Texas**.

coliform bacteria organisms normally found in gastrointestinal system that can invade the prostate; most common type of prostate infection.

collagen protein that occurs naturally in the body; angiostatin and endostatin are taken from collagen and plasminogen: *see* **endostatin**.

color-flow doppler ultrasound (CDUS) ultrasound method that more clearly images tumors by observing the Doppler shift in sound waves caused by the rapid flow of blood through tiny blood vessels that are characteristic of tumors.

combination therapy *see* **combined hormone therapy**.

combined androgen blockade (CAB) testicular androgen suppression plus blockade of adrenal androgens by antiandrogens.

combined hormonal therapy (CHT) use of more than one hormone in therapy: *see* **ADT**, **monotherapy**.

combined modality therapy two or more types of treatment used to supplement each other, for example; surgery, radiation, chemotherapy, hormonal therapy, or immunotherapy may be used alternatively or together for maximum effectiveness.

CombiPatch estrogen and progestin patch used for hormone replacement therapy.

combretastatin A4 (CA4P) (Oxigene): developed from the African willow; may attack proliferating endothelial cells and shut down blood vessels supplying a tumor; *under study.*

complement blood protein capable of killing bacteria and other cells in the presence of an antigen-antibody complex.

complementary therapy *see* **alternative treatment**.

complete blood count (CBC) enumeration of the cellular elements; the red cells (or erythrocytes), white cells (or leukocytes), and platelets (or thrombocytes), along with an evaluation of their adequacy (as to numbers), types (normal, abnormal, precursors), and their ability to function normally.

complete local excision (CLE) complete excision of an entire tumor mass, including a margin of normal tissue that surrounds it, confirmed by histological examination of the margins.

complete response (CR) normalization of the PSA for three successive evaluations, two weeks apart; used in a non-technical urological research plan.

complex prostate specific antigen (cPSA) blood test that can differentiate between prostate cancer and a benign condition; may eliminate the need for early biopsies; *under study.*

compliance abiding with a prescribed regimen; for example, taking one's medicine correctly.

complication unexpected or unwanted effect of a treatment, pharmaceutical, or other procedure.

computed tomography (CT) scan of the pelvis and abdomen is transformed into a 3D view of the contents of the body for this region.

computerized axial tomography (CAT) radioactive transmissions from a radioactive isotope, injected into the body, is evaluated by scanning machines and sent to a computer for image analysis; then projected on a video display.

conformal radiotherapy therapy in which the radiation beam is shaped to target (conformed) to the area of tissue that needs treatment.

conformational therapy therapy that uses careful planning and delivery techniques designed to focus radiation on the areas of the prostate and surrounding tissue that need treatment, and to protect areas that do not need treatment; three-dimensional conformational therapy is a more sophisticated form of this method.

congenital any condition or trait that exists from birth.

conjugated linoleic acid (CLA) isomer of linoleic acid (an essential fatty acid) naturally found in most animals that have been grass-fed; may counteract various cancers.

conservative surgery surgery performed to preserve function or appearance, not to increase survival; may not be as effective as radical surgery in the treatment of malignant tumors.

contracture scarring that can occur at the bladder neck after a radical prostatectomy, resulting in narrowing of the urinary passage between the bladder and the prostatic urethra.

contraindication situation in which a medical treatment is not recommended because of undesirable side effects.

control group in an experimental study, the group of subjects who do not receive the intervention of experimental treatment; the effects of treatment on the experimental group are compared to the effects of no treatment on the control group.

coping strategies mental strategies or behaviors employed to maximize functioning and reduce or eliminate psychological trauma in response to stressful situations.

cordotomy spinal surgery in which bundles of nerves are severed.

core biopsy removal, through a large needle, of a piece of a tumor or lump, called a *core,* then sent to the laboratory to determine if the tumor is benign or malignant.

coriolus versicolor mushroom with antimacrobiotic, antiviral, and antitumor activity attributed to a protein-bound polysaccharide K (PSK): *also known* as **krestin**: *see* **University of Texas**.

corpora cavernosum part of a man's penis that fills with blood when he is sexually excited, giving the organ the stiffness required for intercourse.

corpus cavernosagram test to locate possible leaking veins using a dye which is injected into the penis and then viewed by X-rays.

cortisol hydrocortisone steroid hormone that is released in response to stress; controls the level of glucose, fats, and water in the body and works in preventing the body's normal reaction to disease or damage.

corvus treatment-planning software program that automatically creates an optimal-intensity, modulated treatment plan based on user-specified goals.

couch grass *Graminis rhizoma* herb used for flushing out inflammatory diseases of the urinary tract: *see* **German Commission E**.

Coumadin warfarin (DuPont): drug that prevents blood from clotting.

COX-2 cyclo-oxygenase isoenzyme, involved in the production of prostaglandin; intercellular messenger found in high concentrations at sites of chronic inflammation: *see* **cyclo-oxygenase-2**.

CPS center for patient safety (National Academy of Sciences): proposed organization to establish detailed national goals for reducing medical errors.

CR *see* **complete response**.

CRADA (cooperative research and development agreement): agreement used by two or more firms or a firm with a government agency for cooperative studies.

cranberry fruit *Vaccinium macrocarpon* fruit that may help prevent urinary-tract infections

creatine compound made by the body and used to store energy in the form of phosphate molecules; at that point, it is called *creatine phosphate.*

creatinine part of the blood-chemistry panel test: involves evaluation or the removal of normal waste from protein metabolism; the removal of creatinine is a function of the kidneys.

cross-reaction reaction between an antibody and antigen which crosses lines of specificity.

cryo cold: *see* **cyroablation, cryosurgery,** or **cryotherapy**.

cryoablation *see* **cryosurgery**, and **ablation, hormonal**.

cryosurgery use of liquid nitrogen probes to freeze a particular portion of an organ to extremely low temperatures to kill the tissue prior to surgery, used to destroy cancerous tissue; when used to treat prostate cancer, the cryoprobes are guided by transrectal ultrasound.

cryosurgery techniques methods of cryosurgery which consist of single-freeze, double-freeze, pull-back freeze, follow-up, and retreatment.

cryotherapy *see* **cryosurgery**.

CS clinical stage.

CSAP cryosurgical ablation of the prostate.

Csatary, Laszlo K. Csatary, a medical doctor, discovered a Hungarian farmer with advanced metastatic gastric carcinoma, who had a complete regression after his flock of sheep experienced an epidemic of Newcastle disease; developed a live strain of the Newcastle disease virus and labeled it MTH-68; used primarily in Europe: *see* **University of Texas**.

CT *see* **computed tomography**.

CT-2584 antiangiogenesis drug; *under study*.

CT scan *see* **Cat scan**.

Cunningham clamp two pieces of metal with a piece of sponge rubber glued on each; placed just below the head of the penis, squeezed together and locked in place; used for urinary incontinence.

CUPS cancer of unknown primary site.

curcumin active constituent found in turmeric root of the spice cumin, may inhibit development of certain cancers.

CV 787 (Calydon): potent virus that the manufacturer claims has a kill ratio of one normal cell for every 10,000 cancer cells; *under study*

cycle regular interval of chemotherapy, depending on the type of drug; a cycle starts with the initial administration of the chemotherapy and ends when the nadir has passed and the white blood and platelet counts have returned to pretreatment values; the next cycle may then be started.

cyclin-dependent kinase inhibitor (CDKI) regulator of cell growth, an enzyme inhibitor.

cyclo-oxygenase-2 (COX-2) enzyme that converts arachidonic acid to prostaglandin E2.

Cyclotron particle accelerator that was formally used to deliver proton radiation to treat cancer and currently replaced by the Synchroton; *under study.*

cyproterone acetate *see* **Androcur.**

cystitis inflammation of the urinary bladder.

cystometry procedure in which a catheter is threaded through the urethra into a full bladder to measure the organ's function and pressure dynamics.

cystoscope instrument used by a physician to look inside the urinary bladder and the urethra.

cystoscopy examination of the urinary bladder by insertion of the cystoscope, through the urethra.

cystourethroscopy use of a cystoscope to look inside the bladder and the urethra.

CYT 356 (Cytogen): monoclonal antibody used to deliver a radioactive isotope, (Indium 111), to sites of metastatic prostate cancer; this diagnostic isotope is then detected by a gamma camera to indicate the location and extent of the disease: *see* **Prostascint**.

cytochrome P-450 enzyme for patients who have failed other forms of hormone therapy.

cytokines soluble substance produced by cells to communicate with other cells; includes interferons, interleukins, and tumor necrosis compounds; may boost immune system.

cytology microscopic study of individual cells that have been obtained from surface fluid secretions, or scraped off organs; such preparations are examined for signs of cancer.

cytopathologist specialist in the subspecialty of cellular evaluation; examines prostate cancer smears from fluid or biopsy imprints; best known for examination of PAP smears.

cytoreductive therapy transfer of a gene to a cancer cell; encodes an enzyme that converts a prodrug into a suicide substrate; could eliminate malignant target cells that have been genetically modified: *see* **prodrug**.

cytotoxic drugs drugs that can cause the death of cancer cells; usually refers to drugs used in chemotherapy treatments.

cytoxan active agent in prostate cancer.

D

D diploid

D0-D3 *see* **staging, tumor or cancer**.

dalteparin antiangiogenesis drug; *under study*.

debulking reduction of the volume of cancer by surgery; theory is that any therapy will be more effective when the major volume, or bulk, of the cancer is removed.

D.C. doctor of chiropractic; practitioner who uses physical manipulation and adjustments of the spine for therapy.

Decadron dexamethason (Merck): drug used in conjunction with many different chemotherapies to treat chemotherapy-induced nausea and vomiting.

DeCode genetics (Hoffman LaRoche): investigation, in Iceland, of 12 common hereditary genes in combination with diseases; *under study*.

dehydroepiandrosterone (DHEA) an adrenal androgen; DHEA levels decline with age, yet prostate gland enlargement and cancers increase with age; a sex hormone secreted by the testes that stimulates development of secondary sexual characteristics.

denaturation reversible or irreversible loss of function in proteins and nucleic acids produced by nonphysiological conditions.

dendranthema *Morifolium tzvel* Chinese herb, one of eight in the herbal formula *PC SPES*; its biologic effect is unspecified.

dendrite threadlike, or tree branch-like, extension of a cell.

dendritic cell immune therapy utilizing specialized white blood cells that efficiently present antigen to other cells; such cells are removed from a patient's blood and pulsed in the lab to enhance their activity with prostate-specific membrane antigen (PSMA) peptides, then reinjected into the patient; plays a pivotal role in initiation of immune responses; *under study*.

denial failure to acknowledge some aspect of external reality; an involuntary reaction (as opposed to lying) that aims to avoid anxiety.

deoxypyridinoline (Dpd) bone resorption marker that reflects the breakdown of bone collagen.

deoxyribonucleic acid (DNA or Ploidy DNA) basic biologically active chemical that maintains our genetic codes; may insure healthy cell division; ploidy is a term used to describe the number of sets of chromosomes in a cell.

depo medroxy-progesterone acetate *see* **Depot-Provera**.

Depot-Provera depo medroxyprogesterone acetate (Pharmacia & Upjohn/Schering): long-acting progestin that reduces hot flashes associated with hormonal therapy.

depression pervasive lowering of mood, often associated with tearfulness, sadness, guilt, or irritability; other features include loss of interest in activities, lowered energy levels, impaired concentration, and disturbance of sleep and/or appetite.

DES *see* **diethylstilbestrol**.

detail person pharmaceutical company sales representative who frequently leaves product samples with physicians.

Detrol tolterodine (Pharmacia & Upjohn): drug used to treat overactive bladder, including symptoms of urinary frequency, urgency, or urge incontinence.

DEXA *see* **dual energy X-ray absorptiometry**.

dexamethasone *see* **Decadron**.

dexascan low exposure X-ray to test the density of the spine and hip; used to evaluate osteoporosis.

DFS disease-free survival.

DHA docosahexaenoic acid, a long-chain fatty acid contained in fish oils.

DHEA *see* **dehydroepiandrosterone**.

DHEA-S DHEA-sulfate, the more stable metabolite of DHEA.

DHT *see* **dihydrotestosterone**.

DI diploid index; *see* **diploid**.

diabetes insipidus disease of the pituitary gland or kidney; called "water diabetes;" characterized by excessive urine excretion, thirst and hunger, and the feeling of weakness.

diagnosis identification and evaluation of signs, symptoms, and selected test results by a physician to determine the causes of the signs and symptoms, and whether a specific disease or disorder is involved.

diaphoresis profuse perspiration.

DIC *see* **disseminated intravascular coagulation**.

Didronel etidronate/disodium (Procter & Gamble): drug used to treat osteoporosis and bone metabolism problems.

diet what a person usually eats or drinks; role of the diet in the prevention and treatment of prostate cancer; there is no credible evidence to show that diet can prevent prostate cancer; diet can affect the progression of the disease.

dietary intervention although studies indicate that populations with low-fat, high-fiber diets have a lower prostate cancer incidence, no studies have shown that a change to a low fat diet lowers prostate cancer after years of a high-fat diet.

dietary supplement product intended to supplement the diet; may contain one or more of the following ingredients: vitamin, mineral, amino acid, herb, or other botanical not represented as a conventional food or as a sole item of a meal or the diet.

diethylstilbestrol (DES) synthetic analog of the female hormone estrogen; formerly used as an option to surgical castration.

dietitian specialist in nutrition, whose role is planning meals; may recommend recipes, vitamins, and nutritional supplements.

differential blood test that shows the number of various types of white cells in the circulating blood.

differentiation evaluation of the differences between normal and prostate cancer cells, as seen under the microscope; a term used to grade the severity of the disease: *well differentiated cells* closely resemble normal cells, while *poorly differentiated cells* are abnormal, malignant, and may be difficult to classify as tumor cells belonging to a particular cell group.

difluoromethylornithine (DFMO) chemopreventive agent present in a variety of animal tumors that may affect cell proliferation and cell differentiation; *under study.*

digest: *see* **PC digest**.

digital rectal examination (DRE) rectal examination by a physician in which a gloved and lubricated finger is inserted into the rectum; used to screen for abnormalities of the prostate and rectum; the physician palpates (feels) the prostate gland through the rectal wall; the presence of lumps or hard areas indicate possible prostate cancer. It is recommended to wait at least one week after a DRE before drawing blood for a PSA.

dihydrotestosterone (DHT) 5 alpha male hormone that is most active in the prostate; it is made when an enzyme in the prostate stimulates the transformation of testosterone to DHT.

5 alpha reductase.

dimethylxanthenone acetic acid antiangiogenesis drug in clinical trial; *under study*.

DIN diploid index number.

dionaea muscipula *see* **carnivora**.

dioxychlor (American Biologics, Mexico): nontoxic oxidative agent.

diphosphonate analog that suppresses bone resorption and mineralization of osteoclasts, the cells that break down bone-cell growth in bony tissue.

diploid (DIP) having one complete set of normally paired chromosomes, (i.e., a normal amount of DNA); diploid cancer cells tend to grow slowly and respond well to hormone therapy; *see* **aneuploid, tetraploid**.

discipline field of study.

disease-free survival elapsed time from the primary treatment of cancer to the first evidence of its recurrence.

disseminated intravascular coagulation (DIC) widespread blood clotting, possibly caused by metastatic cancer or its treatment.

disseminated prostate cancer cancer found throughout the prostate gland or widely in the body as metastases.

Ditropan XL oxybutynin chloride (Hoechst Marion Roussel/Alza): drug used to treat overactive bladder.

diuretics drugs that help rid the body of excess water through frequent urination.

DMP dionaea muscipula plant: *see* **carnivora**.

DNA type of code, with four different chemical bases arranged in endless combinations, to form genetic blueprints.

DNA ploidy analysis through static cytometry pathological analysis that may determine the ploidy patterns from a sample of tissue obtained from a fine- needle aspiration biopsy. This test compares the number of chromosomes and the DNA in a normal cell; may indicate whether the cell has the potential for fast or slow growth.

DNA-ploidy DNA *see* **deoxyribonucleic acid**.

DNA probe short segment of DNA whose base sequence is specifically complementary to a particular gene segment.

D.O. doctor of osteopathy; physician who uses manipulative, as well as the diagnostic and therapeutic measures, of conventional medicine.

DOA dead on arrival; status for persons who die before reaching the hospital.

DOB date of birth.

Doclitaxel and estramustine (NCI-V99-1546): used as a combination chemotherapy in patients with hormone refractory prostate cancer; *under study*.

docs physicians.

DOD date of death.

dolasetron mesylate *see* **Anzemet**.

D.O.M. doctor of oriental medicine; usually proficient in acupuncture.

dominant gene gene that usually results in a specific disease, even though the individual's genome possesses only one copy.

Doppler study that shows blood flow and velocity in normal and abnormal blood vessels; may uncover increased blood flow required by growing cancers.

Doppler, color computerized display of Doppler shown in color.

Doppler, power highly sensitive form of color Doppler; shows blood flow and velocity in normal and abnormal blood vessels as well as detecting the increased blood flow by growing prostate cancer.

dormant growth arrested state; researchers at Memorial Sloan-Kettering found that withdrawal of testosterone caused a majority of the tumor cells to go into a dormant state.

dosage amount of a therapeutic substance.

dose amount of a therapeutic substance to be taken during a specified time period.

dose-response relationship relationship in which a change in the amount, duration, or intensity of an exposure to a drug is associated with an increase or decrease in an outcome, or risk of an outcome.

dosimetrist technician who carefully calculates the dose of radiation and develops a number of treatment plans to make certain that the tumor gets enough radiation.

Dostinex cabergolin (Pharmacia & Upjohn): prolactin-lowering agent that increases the number of androgen receptors.

double-blind study form of clinical trial in which neither the physician nor the patient knows the actual treatment that any individual patient is receiving; double-blind trials are a way of minimizing the influence of the placebo effect as well as the personal opinions of patients and physicians on the results of the trial.

double helix two strands of DNA wound around the other; as the cells divide to form two identical cells, the double helix unwinds and makes a copy of itself; using , each strand of DNA can make a copy of itself forming a new double helix.

doubling time the time that it takes a particular focus of cancer to double in size.

downsizing use of hormonal or other forms of management to reduce the volume of prostate cancer in and/or around the prostate prior to attempted curative treatment.

downstaging use of hormonal or other forms of management in the attempt to lower the clinical stage of prostate cancer prior to attempted curative treatment; (e.g., from stage T3a to T2b); this technique is highly controversial.

doxazosin *see* **Cardura**.

doxorubicin *see* **Adriamycin.**

dpd *see* **deoxypyridinoline**.

DRE *see* **digital rectal examination**.

drip collector internal or external device to collect urine from an incontinent person.

drug interaction clinically significant actions or influences of one medication upon the effectiveness or toxicity of another.

dry ejaculation see **retro ejaculation**.

dual energy X-ray absorption (DEXA) bone-marrow density scan.

ductal carcinoma cancer that occurs in the prostate duct, mammary (breast) glands, pancreas and salivary glands.

duplication production of a copy of a gene or a chromosome.

Duros leuprolide (Alza): drug-filled titanium implant, when placed under the skin of a patient's arm; can deliver drug continuously for up to 12 months; *under study*.

DV daily value.

DVT deep venous thrombosis.

dyspareunia pain or discomfort during sexual intercourse.

dysplasia abnormal growth of cells that have some of the features of carcinoma, but insufficient changes to warrant a diagnosis of carcinoma: *see* **atypia**, **PIN**.

dyspnea shortness of breath, difficult breathing.

dysuria problematic or painful urination.

Dx diagnosis.

DXA *see* **dual-energy X-ray absorptiometry**.

E

early detection disease found at an early stage, before it has grown or spread to other sites.

EB 1089 vitamin D analogue for post prostatectomy patients with early recurrence as indicated by a rising PSA; currently used in treatment of breast cancer; *under study*.

EBR, **EBRT** external beam radiation: *see* **external beam radiation therapy**.

e-cadherin gene that may be involved in the development and progression of prostate cancer.

ECG, EGCG *Epicatechin gallate, Epigallocatechin gallat* major components of green tea, representing about 30 percent of the dry weight of a hot water extract of green tea; both components can prevent activation of the male hormones needed for the development of cancer.

echinacea purpurea root *Echinacea pururea radix* used for infections of the urinary tract; may have immune effects that increase the number of white blood cells; recent studies indicate that echinacea may also change genetic material in sperm viability: *see* **German Commission E**, **Not approved**; the echinacea purpurea leaf is approved by the German Commission..

EchoGen 851 (Sonus): fluorocarbon-based contrast agent being developed for the detection of prostate cancer; *under study.*

EcoGen brand name for a soybean isoflavone (genistein, daidzein, and glycitein) concentrate.

ED *see* **erectile dysfunction**.

edema swelling or accumulation of fluid in some part of the body.

Edex alprostadil (Schwarz): drug used to treat erectile dysfunction; administered via injection.

EFA *see* **essential fatty acids**.

efficacy extent to which, under ideal conditions, an intervention, procedure, regimen, or treatment, produces a benefit.

EGF epidermal growth compound; a protein known to activate the endothelial cell; *see* **endothelial cells** and **VEGF**.

eicosanoids substances produced by the body during inflammation.

ejaculate release of semen during orgasm.

ejaculation discharging of semen through the penis during orgasm. Note: ejaculation up to 24-48 hours before a PSA test can affect the PSA level.

ejaculatory ducts tubular passages through which semen reaches the prostatic urethra during orgasm.

EKG electrocardiogram: *also called* **ECG**.

electrolytes substances, which in solution, are capable of conveying an electric current; in the blood plasma, these include ions of sodium, potassium, chlorides, bicarbonates, etc.

electrophoresis technique that separates DNA by weight, for analysis, by leaving hundreds of types of genetic material on a strip of film.

electrostimulation mild electrical current that may stimulate ejaculation; also used to strengthen muscle action to control voiding in incontinent persons: *also may be called* **electroejaculation**.

ELISA *see* **enzyme-linked immunosorbent assay**.

ellagic acid substance found in raspberries, strawberries, walnuts, and other plants; being evaluated for anticancer activity.

Elmiron pentosan polysulfate sodium (Alza): drug that relieves bladder pain or discomfort associated with interstitial cystitis..

embolism blood clot.

Emcyt estramustine phosphat (Pharmacia & Upjohn): chemotherapeutic combination of estrogen and mechlorethamine that appears to interfere with the growth of cancer cells; used in conjunction with Taxotere or Taxol for late-stage prostate cancer.

Emcyt/taxotere chemotherapy combination; *under study.*

Emcyt/taxotere/carboplatin chemotherapy combination; *under study.*

emission initial phase of the male orgasm.

EMP hybrid drug combination of nitrogen mustard and estrogen that disrupts cytoplasmic (an intercellular serine proteinase) microtubules (made of protein).

endocrine glands structures in the body whose secretions flow directly into the bloodstream and are immediately mediated.

endocrine therapy treatment that affects the release or action of a hormone in the body.

endocrinologist specialist of the endocrine glands and hormone systems of the body; for example; pituitary gland, adrenal gland, testes.

endogenous produced from within and inherent naturally to an organism.

endonuclease enzyme that splits bonds.

endorectal MRI magnetic resonance imaging in which a long narrow tube containing radio-frequency coils is inserted into the rectum; this technique provides a clearer picture of the prostate gland than does the standard MRI; *see* **magnetic resonance imaging**.

endorphin compound which may block the cancer cell opiate receptors and prevent the cell from receiving messages to divide; prostate cancer has an opiate receptor.

Endostatin (EntreMed): anti-angiogenic substance that is a fragment of two larger proteins, collagen and plasminogen, that occur naturally in the body; it has successfully shrunk tumors in mice without recurrence after the drug has been stopped; *under study.*

endothelial cells cells that line the surface of the walls of blood vessels; source of new blood vessels with an ability to divide and migrate: *see* **aFGF, bFGF, EGF.**

enlarged prostate prostate that grows beyond its normal size and presses against the urethra preventing the free flow of the urine.

Entelev *see* **CanCell.**

enucleate to separate and remove from surrounding tissue; during prostate-removal surgery, the surgeon enucleates the prostate gland from the tissue around it.

enuresis nocturna bed-wetting.

enzyme any protein that acts as a catalyst, increasing the rate of a chemical reaction within the body without being changed itself; enzyme names often end with the suffix - *ase.*

enzyme-linked immunosorbent assay (ELISA) laboratory method used to detect the presence of antibodies and antigens.

EOD extent of disease.

eosinophils type of white blood cell, found in the circulating blood; associated with allergic disorders, parasitic infestations, etc.

EPA eicosopentaenoic acid, a long-chain fatty acid present in fish oils.

epidemiology study of the relationships of the factors that affect the cause, course, and outcome of a disease within or throughout a population group.

epidermis outermost layer of skin.

epididymis structure in which sperm is stored after it is made in the testicles.

epididymitis infection of tubal structures surrounding the testicles.

epidural anesthesia injection of anesthetic into the space around the spinal column; the amount of pain relief can be adjusted while the patient remains conscious.

epidural dorsal stimulation surgical implantation of electrodes over the spinal cord; the patient applies electrical impulses when required.

epithelial cells cells that cover the surface of the body and line its cavities.

EPO *see* **erythroprotein**.

epoetin alfa *see* **epogen**.

Epogen epoetin alfa (Amgen/Johnson & Johnson): a glycoprotein that stimulates red blood cell production; a synthetic form of a natural hormone called erythropoietin; *see* **erythropoietin**.

epothilones factor, similar to the yew tree compound, that may interfere with the ability of cancer cells to divide; *under study.*

EPS *see* **expressed prostatic secretion**.

ER *see* **estrogen receptor**.

erectile dysfunction (ED) consistent inability to achieve and/or maintain an erection sufficient for sexual activity: *see* **impotence**.

Erectogenic oral drug used as an aid in erectile dysfunction.

ER/MRI endorectal magnetic resonance imaging.

ER/MRSI endorectal magnetic resonance spectroscope imaging; imaging process that uses a magnetic resonance of atoms in body tissues to produce cross-sectional, and even three-dimensional images of internal organs; inserted through the rectum.

ERUS endorectal ultrasound

eryngo *Eryngium campestre* herb used in the treatment of urinary-tract infections.

erythema redness of the skin; may be the earliest sign of radiation reaction; may also be due to skin irritation due to various causes.

erythrocyte hemoglobin-containing red blood cell in the circulating blood; transports and delivers oxygen from the lungs to the body tissues.

erythrocyte count *see* **red cell count.**

erythropoietin (EPO) protein normally produced by the kidneys that stimulates the bone marrow to produce red blood cells.

escherichia coli ***E. col*** common coliform bacteria: *see* **coliform bacteria**.

essential fatty acids (EFA) the three fatty acids required for growth in mammals: arachidonic, linolenic and linoleic acids; only linoleic acids need to be supplied in the diet; the additional two can be made from it: *see* **linoleic acid**.

essiac herb for cancer patients: *also known* as **Ezzeac Plus**, a modified essiac product: *see* **University of Texas**.

Esteem (Imagyn): brand name of a vacuum device for erectile dysfunction.

extracorporeal magnetic innervation (ExMI) (Neotonus/Mayo Clinic): therapeutic procedure that uses pulsing magnetic fields to strengthen the pelvic floor muscles that affect bladder control; *under study.*

estradiol transdermal *see* **Climara.**

estramustine phosphate may inhibit cell growth in the hormone-resistant human prostate cancer cell line DU 145; used in conjunction with other drugs; *under study*: *see* **Emcyt**.

Estratab (Solvay): low-dose estrogen treatment used to prevent osteoporosis.

estrogen female sex hormone essential for the development of secondary sex characteristics, such as breasts; certain estrogens, (e.g., diethylstilbestrol), are used in the treatment of prostate cancer.

estrogen-like exerting biological effects similar to that of estrogen.

estrogen receptor (ER) intracellular receptor protein that binds estrogens and antiestrogens to DNA and alters the expression of specific genes; it is an indicator of responsiveness to hormonal therapies; high ER expression is associated with a good prognosis and with a positive response to hormonal therapy.

estrogen receptor assay (ER-ICA) test of cancerous tissue to determine whether it is hormone-dependent and thus may respond to hormonal therapy; test results express whether the cancer is ER positive or negative; currently limited to breast cancer tumor models.

estrogens/medroxyprogesterone acetate; *see* **PremPro**.

ET-1 endothelin-1, prostate cell product that may be responsible for bone pain in metastatic prostate cancer.

ET/CD Emcyt taxotere/carboplatin decadron, a chemotherapy program.

ethanol *see* **alcohol, absolute**.

ethnobotanical study to identify the active molecules in folk remedies, so that they may be made into modern prescription drugs; so far, results have been unsuccessful.

ethylenediaminetetra acetic acid *see* **chelation therapy**.

etidronate *see* **bisphosphonates**.

etidronate/disodium *see* **Didronel**.

etiocholanolone sex hormone secreted by the testes.

etiology (etiol) cause of disease or the study of causes of disease.

etoposide *see* **VP-16**.

Eulexin flutamide (Schering): drug used in the treatment of metastatic prostate cancer.

euploid balanced set of chromosomes in any number.

evidence-based medicine treatments whose value is established beyond a reasonable doubt.

Evista raloxifene (Eli Lilly): drug used to prevent osteoporosis.

E vitamin (University of Wisconsin-Madison): when used with R 1881, a synthetic male hormone, it appears to counteract some of the negative effects of male hormones on prostate cells linked to the development of prostate cancer; *under study*.

EWB emotional well-being.

excisional biopsy surgical removal of tissue for diagnosis of disease; such as tumors.

exercise regular series of movements that has many benefits including a reduced risk of blood clots and osteoporosis.

exisulind *see* **Aptosyn**, **LNCap**.

exogenous glands (exocrine glands) glands whose secretions flow through a duct system and are released as needed.

experimental unproven (or even untested) technique or procedure; certain experimental treatments are commonly used in the management of prostate cancer.

expressed prostatic secretion (EPS) prostatic fluid that is obtained by gentle massage of the prostate during a digital rectal examination.

expressed sequence tags (ESTs) *see* **messenger RNA**.

external beam radiation therapy (EBRT) radiation therapy in which the radiation is delivered by a machine pointed at the area to be radiated.

external collection device system used to collect urine from an incontinent person.

external urethral sphincter muscle ring-like band of muscle fibers that contract when the patient wants to stop urinating; these fibers act as an involuntary mechanism of continence following a radical prostatectomy.

extra capsular extension condition in which a tumor has invaded and extended through and beyond the prostatic capsule (the membranous covering of the prostate gland) indicating a more advanced stage of the disease.

extracapsular prostate tissue tissue that immediately surrounds the outside of the prostate; if the cancer has spread to this area or beyond, it is considered to be advanced disease.

extraprostatic extending through the capsule of the prostate into the surrounding tissue.

eyes *see* **iridology**.

F

fab antigen-binding fragment of the antibody molecule; this portion determines the antigen specificity of the antibody.

false negative erroneous negative test results; for example, an imaging test that fails to show the presence of a tumor later found by biopsy to be present in the patient, is said to be a false negative result.

false positive positive test result mistakenly identifying a state or condition that does not in fact exist.

family history in relation to prostate cancer, studies show that the risk of prostate cancer increases two to three times for men who have a family history of the disease.

fascia flat layers of fibrous tissue that separate different layers of tissue.

Fc crystallizable fragment of the antibody molecule; this portion determines effector functions of the antibody.

FCE 26644, FCE 26950 antiangiogenesis drugs; *under study.*

fear to be afraid of, to dread; with localized prostate cancer, fear is for metastasis; with metastasized prostate cancer, fear is for the formation of tumors of the bone; final fear is for the prostate cancer to become androgen independent (hormone refractory).

fecal incontinence involuntary loss of stool at least once a week: *see* **Acticon**.

FFA free fatty acid.

FGFR2 fibroblast growth compound receptor 2, genetic switch in prostate cancer cells that triggers a quiescent tumor to erupt into an invasive, deadly cancer: hopefully, this discovery will lead to new drugs to kill cancer cells; *under study.*

fibrosis soft tissue scarring which may take place after radiation therapy.

Finasteride (NCI/Merck): compound used to treat benign prostatic hyperplasia, being tested to see if it can prevent or treat prostate cancer; *under study*: *see* **Proscar**.

fine needle aspiration use of a thin needle to withdraw tissue from the body; in the case of suspected prostate cancer, it is used in conjunction with a transrectal ultrasound.

fingerprinted term used by some herbal product manufacturers to indicate the purity of the product.

FISH fluorescence in situ hybridization (Mayo Clinic): process which paints chromosomes or portions of chromosomes with fluorescent molecules; useful for gene mapping; may be useful in predicting disease progression; *under study.*

fish oils studies indicate that fish oil plays a positive role in the prevention and treatment of colon cancer by inhibiting angiogenesis, the growth of new blood vessels that supply nutrients essential for cancer cell growth.

fissures cracks in the anal canal, caused by hard bowel movements or by an inflammation of the colon, which can cause anal bleeding and severe pain.

fistula epithelial-lined passage or tunnel formed in the body congenitally, by disease or injury, or occasionally by surgery or radiation, leading from one internal organ to another or from an internal organ to the body's exterior; the most common is *anal fistula.*

flank pain pain commonly related to an abnormality of the kidney.

flare reaction (flare) temporary increase in tumor growth and symptoms caused by some LHRH agonists; can be mild to dangerous; may be prevented by taking an antiandrogen (Casodex or Eulexin), several days before starting an LHRH agonist (Lupron or Zoladex),: *also known as a* **biochemical flare**.

flavonoid antioxidant that may prevent various cancers; sources are grape seed, green tea and cayenne.

flaxseed plain flaxseed is high in plant estrogens, which may account for their possible benefits against prostate cancer; there is also evidence that flax seed oil may enhance the growth of prostate cancer.

Flomax tamsulosin (Boehringer Ingelheim): drug used to relax the prostate and bladder neck to improve urine flow and to reduce bladder obstruction in benign prostatic: *see* **alpha-1-adrenergic blockers**.

Flor-Essence herbal tonic commercial, herbal extract, essiac tea blend: *see* **University of Texas**.

flow cytometry technique that determines the fraction of cells that are normal (diploid) from abnormal (tetraploid, aneuploid, etc.).

fluoroscopy technique in which a moving X-ray image is used to view the lower urinary tract before and after treatment.

flutamide *see* **Eulexin**.

foam mold a plastic mold of the legs to maintain the correct position for a patient being given radiation therapy; *also called* **alpha cradle**.

focal prostate cancer cancer found in only a few small areas of the prostate.

Foley catheter tube inserted into the urethra and bladder through the tip of the penis; can be used to drain urine from the bladder or to irrigate the bladder and prostatic urethra to prevent the formation of blood clots.

folic acid, or folate part of the B-complex family; *sometimes referred to as* **vitamin M**; a coenzyme required for the synthesis of RNA and DNA, the nucleic acids used for healthy cell division.

follicle-stimulating hormone (FSH) hormone that stimulates sperm production in the testicles, or other glands containing follicles.

foot *see* **reflexology**.

Fosamax alendronate sodium (Merck): bisphosphonate that inhibits bone breakdown; also shown to suppress tumors.

fosfomycin trometamol *see* **Monurol**.

FR-111142 antiangiogenesis drug; *under study*.

free PSA *see* **Prostate Specific Antigen Type II**.

frequency the need to urinate often.

fresh cell therapy alternative treatment that involves injections of fresh embryonic animal cells taken from the organ or tissue that corresponds to the unhealthy organ or tissue in the patient; proponents claim that the body automatically transports the injected cells to the target organ where they repair and recondition the sick cells: *also known as* **live cell therapy** or **cellular therapy**.

frozen section technique in which excised tissue is frozen, cut into thin slices, and stained for microscopic examination; since a pathologist can rapidly complete a frozen section analysis, the procedure is commonly used during surgery to quickly provide the surgeon with a preliminary pathologic opinion of whether prostate cancer is present in the gland, and, usually in the pelvic lymph nodes.

FSH *see* **follicle-stimulating hormone**.

FUD factor fear, uncertainty and doubt of a patient who receives a diagnosis of prostate cancer.

functional incontinence incontinence in a person unable to reach the toilet in time due to disorientation, confusion, or communication problems.

FUO fever of unknown origin.

G

G Gleason score.

gadolinium nonradioactive substance injected into the body to enhance the ability to visualize abnormalities during magnetic resonance imaging (MRI).

gamma globulin immunoglobulin of the IgG subclass that plays a major role in the process of immunity: *see* **IgG**.

gamma glutamyl transpedtidase (GGT) part of the blood-chemistry panel test: an enzyme involved in the function of the liver, heart, and muscle cells; measured for toxic effects of therapy (drugs).

gamma knife form of radiation therapy that uses a highly focused beam.

ganglia group of nerve cell bodies.

ganoderma lucidum Chinese herb, one of eight in the herbal formula *PC SPES*, contains high molecular weight polysaccharide (complex sugar) compounds that may inhibit the growth of sarcoma-37 cancer cell lines.

garlic *Allium sativum* herb that possibly contains an enzyme important to forming cancer-preventing allyl sulfur compounds: *see* **German Commission E**, **University of Texas**.

gastrointestinal related to the digestive system; stomach, intestines, etc.

Gatorade brand-name beverage containing carbohydrates and minerals that *PC SPES* users drink to replace lost electrolytes and to reduce symptoms of leg cramping that may be caused by an electrolyte deficiency.

GBC-590 (SafeScience): complex non-toxic carbohydrate compound; may arrest tumor growth and shrink tumors; *under study.*

GCSF *see* **granulocyte colony stimulating compound**.

gene basic unit of heredity located on chromosomes.

gene amplification increased copy number per cell of an individual gene.

gene expression specific process in which a gene is switched on at a certain time, and begins production of its protein.

gene mapping process to determine the relative positions of genes on a chromosome and the distance between them.

gene, orphan gene that has been deciphered but whose function is still unknown.

gene reporters gene injected with the therapeutic gene to monitor the effectiveness of the therapeutic gene.

gene testing examining a sample of blood, other body fluid, or tissue for biochemical, or genetic markers, that indicate the presence or absence of genetic disease.

gene therapy treatment of disease by genetic modification of the cells; toxic genes are injected into a cancer point to destroy cancer cells or to replace a faulty gene with a good gene to correct a disease. As of 1999, more than 2,000 people have received gene therapy; 331 studies have received FDA approval; *under study: see* **Human Genome Project** and **Genset**.

gene therapy vaccine (John Hopkins): preparation of cancer cells from each individual patient; initial tests showed activation of the entire immune system to fight the cancer; *under study.*

genetically engineered (GE) term used to refer to food that is created by the splicing of genes from various species of plants, animals, bacteria or viruses into different species of fruits, grains, and vegetables; the Food and Drug Administration does not require safety testing for adverse reactions of GE foods.

genetically engineered vaccine vaccine which contains genes encoded for proteins found in tumors; the vaccine prompts an immune response against the tumor cells; *see* autologous and allogenic.

genetic code instructions in a gene to make a specific protein. DNA code letters are a (adenine), t (thymine), g (guanine) and t (thymine); make up the nucleotide bases of DNA.

genetic drift growing cancer may "drift" from a well-differentiated, slow-growing tumor to a poorly differentiated, aggressive malignancy.

genetic marker portion of DNA with an identifiable physical location on a chromosome; permits inheritance to be followed.

genetics scientific study of heredity; how particular qualities or traits are transmitted from parents to offspring.

genetic screening identification of a population group to find individuals at high risk for transmitting a specific genetic disorder.

gene transfer insertion of an unrelated DNA into the cells of an organism to treat a disease.

genistein nutrient found in soy protein that may inhibit the formation of prostate tumors; initial experiments indicate that genistein may have a role in therapy as well as prevention.

genital system biological system which, in males, includes the testes, seminal vesicles, the vas deferens, the prostate, and the penis.

genitofemoral nerve abdominal nerve used by a plastic surgeon to replace damaged or removed cavernous nerves during a radical prostatectomy or a radical retropubic prostatectomy.

genitourinary related to the genital and urinary tract.

genitourinary system combined genital and urinary systems; *also known* as the **genitourinary tract**.

GENN genetically engineered neural network: *see* **quantitative nuclear grade**.

genome all the DNA contained in a cell or organism.

Genset (Synthelab, Abbott, Johnson and Johnson): analysis of human genes to find links with common diseases; the goal is developing drugs to cure such diseases; *under study*.

gerancol an oil in the skin that may curtail tumor growth.

German Commission E herbal watchdog government agency in Germany, must approve herbs before physicians can write prescriptions for them. If the description of a herb in this *Reference Guide* says **Not Approved,** then it indicates that the Commission considered the item and did not approve it for public use. If the description of a herb in this *Reference Guide* says *see* **German Commission E**; it indicates that the Commission studied the item and approved it for use in patients.

Gerson clinic *see* **Govallo, Valentin I**.

Gerson, Max B. Gerson developed a dietary program in the 1940s consisting of sodium and potassium water intake, frequent consumption of fruit and vegetable juices, strict dietary fat reduction, temporary restriction of protein, with a vegetarian diet and frequent coffee enemas; the program is reported to improve general health and well-being.

GG Gleason's grade.

GGT *see* **gamma glutamyl transpedtidase**.

GI gastrointestinal.

ginseng root found mainly in Asia; animal studies are under way to determine if Korean red ginseng saponins can modulate carcinogenic metabolism and impact the progression of established and developing cancerous lesions in the rat colon.

gland structure or organ which produces a substance that may be used locally, or in another part of the body; *see* **endocrine glands** and **exogenous glands**.

Gleason, D.F. pathologist who developed the Gleason score method of grading prostate cancer.

Gleason grading system of describing the degree of aggressiveness of prostate cancer based on the appearance of the cancer cells.

Gleason score widely used method for classifying the cellular differentiation of cancerous tissues; the less the cancerous cells appear like normal cells, the more malignant the cancer. Two numbers, each from 1 to 5, are assigned successively to the two predominant patterns of differentiation present in the examined tissue sample; added together, these produce the Gleason score. Low numbers of 2, 3, 4 indicate a well differentiated cancer; 5, 6 indicate a moderately well differentiated cancer and grade 7 is considered significant. High numbers, (i.e., 8, 9, 10), indicate poor differentiation and a disease with a more aggressive clinical behavior.

globo H-KLH carbohydrate molecule found in large numbers on the surface of many cancer cells; a vaccine treatment for men with refractory prostate cancer; *under study.*

globulin part of the blood-chemistry panel test: a protein fraction; elevated globulin levels may indicate chronic infection.

glucosamine, N acetyl may ease pain of osteroporosis resulting from taking hormones; do not use with chrondroitin.

glucose part of the blood-chemistry panel test and the complete blood count test; a measure of sugar content in the blood.

glucosuria glucose in the urine.

glutamine one of the nonessential amino acids.

glycyrrhiza glabra, uralensis Chinese herb, one of eight in the herbal formula *PC SPES*; contains saponins that may stimulate the immune system and inhibit the expression of the Epstein-Barr virus (associated with the development of certain cancers); has anticancer activities when tested in the laboratory; glycyrrhiza is metabolically converted to glycyrrhetic acid when incubated in the laboratory with adrenal gland cells; increases DHEA production.

GM 1474 antiangiogenesis drug; *under study.*

GM2 ganglioside molecule that may serve as a target for immune recognition and attack; *under study*: *see* **allogenic**.

GM-CSF Granulocyte-macrophage colony-stimulating compound gene, that produces a protein, that when added to cancer cells, divides the cancer cells and presents them to T-cells, which kill them. The T-cells continue to kill any cells that carry the tumor antigen; this process is called targeted therapy; *under study: see* **T-cells**.

gm/dl, g/dl grams per deciliter; used to measure concentration of substances in the blood.

GnRH gonadotropin-releasing hormone.

goldenrod *Solidago virga-aurea* herb bearing yellow flowers that is used as an irrigation therapy for diseases of the lower urinary tract: *see* **German Commission E**.

gonadotropin hormone, secreted from the pituitary gland, stimulates growth of the gonads and secretion of sex hormones, including follicle-stimulating hormone and luteinizing hormone.

gonads organ that produces sex cells, such as the testis and the ovaries.

gonorrhea infection caused by a microorganism which may infect the prostate; characterized by a yellowish color discharge from the penis.

Gonzalez, Nicholas, M.D. Gonzalez offers alternative treatment including ten basic diets with as many as 90 variations, coffee enemas, and up to 150 pills a day; used a test of a patient's hair for treatment and was sued in 1997.

goserelin acetate *see* **Zoladex**.

Govallo, Valentin I, M.D. Govallo pioneered an alternative treatment of cancer patients in 1975 using an extract of chorionic villi from placentas taken after live, full-term deliveries; claims that this treatment is most effective when administered after surgery and before chemotherapy or radiotherapy; practiced at the Immune Augmentative Therapy (IAT) clinic in Freeport, Bahamas, and the Gerson Clinic in Tijuana, Mexico: *see* **University of Texas**.

GP general practitioner.

g proteins guanidine nuculeotide-binding proteins that regulate a variety of signal transduction trails, including the alpha-1 smooth muscle response within the prostate.

grade means of describing the potential degree of severity of a cancer based on the microscopic appearance of cancer cells: a grade 1 carcinoma is well differentiated and associated with a good prognosis; a grade 2 is moderately differentiated and associated with intermediate prognosis; a grade 3 is poorly differentiated and associated with a poor prognosis. Tumors are low, intermediate, or high grades: *see* **Gleason score**.

granisetron hydrochloride *see* **Kytril**.

granulocyte colony stimulating compound (GCSF) compound which helps recovery of white blood cells in the bone marrow from radiation or chemotherapy.

granulocytes subset of white blood cells; these cells include neutrophils, eosinophils, and basophils, and are collectively known as *polymorphonuclear leukocytes;* part of the immune system.

gray *(Gy)* 100 rads. The unit of radiation dosage; used in therapeutic cancer management usually vary from 45 to 65 gray; a *centigray* is 1/100 of a gray.

greater bindweed *Calystegia sepiu* was used for urinary-tract diseases; extremely strong action and not in use.

Greek cancer cure Dr. Hariton-Tzannis Alivizatos, of Greece, claimed to have perfected a blood test that could determine the type, location and severity of any cancer; also claimed that he had a serum that let the patient's immune system destroy cancer cells.

green tea *Camellia sinensis* components may be effective in activation of male hormones; compounds may be affected and diminished when taken in capsule form; used for stomach disorders: *see* **University of Texas**.

grief normal emotional response to loss, which may include a complex range of painful feelings such as sadness, anger, helplessness, guilt, and despair.

growth compounds molecules in the body that can possibly increase the amount of cell division leading to growth; may also stimulate cancer growth.

GS *see* **Gleason score**.

GSS Gleason sum score; the most common grade of tumor as seen by the first number of the Gleason score.

GTP green tea polyphenol; the active substance within green tea.

GU system genitourinary system, the organ system that deals with the reproductive and urinary systems of the body.

GVAX prostate cancer vaccine that induces specific anti-tumor immunity against tumor antigens on the gene-modified prostate cancer cells; a form of gene therapy; *under study.*

gynecomastia enlargement or tenderness of breast tissue in males; may be a side effect of hormonal therapy.

H

Haelon 951 fermented soybean oral nutritional beverages.

half-life period of time required for an isotope's radioactivity to decay to half its original strength.

HAMA *see* **human anti-mouse (or murine) antibody**.

haploid containing half the diploid number of chromosomes and only one of each kind of chromosome.

Hayflick limit *see* **telomeres**.

HB *see* **hormone blockade**.

HCE hypercoagulable event.

Hct *see* **hematocrit.**

HDC high dose chemotherapy.

HDK high dose ketoconazole: *see* **Nizoral**.

HDL cholesterol high-density lipoprotein, which is referred to as the "good" cholesterol; a transport protein that carries cholesterol away from the artery walls for removal from the body; the higher the HDL value, the lower the risk of cardiovascular disease; part of the blood-chemistry panel test.

HDR *see* **high dose rate**.

heather *Calluna vulgaris* herb used as a diuretic for diseases and ailments of the kidneys and

hemangiomas congenital tumors of the blood vessels; benign but are often fatal.

hematocrit (Hct) part of the complete blood count test; the percentage or volume of red blood cells in whole blood; low hematocrit levels are associated with certain types of anemia.

hematologist physician specializing in the treatment of blood diseases.

hematology study of blood, blood-forming tissues, and diseases of the blood and their treatment.

hematopoiesis process by which blood cells are formed and developed.

hematospermia occurrence of blood in the semen.

hematuria occurrence of blood in the urine.

hemodialysis method of removing waste products from the blood when the kidney is unable to do so.

hemoglobin (Hgb) part of the complete blood count test; oxygen-carrying component in the red blood cells; low results are usually associated with certain types of anemia.

hemostasis arrest of bleeding.

Heparin (Abbott): anticoagulant that prevents blood from clotting; available from different mucopolysaccharides of animal origin

hepatotoxicity toxic effects on the liver.

her-2 human epidermal growth compound receptor-2; a protein that prompts cells to reproduce out of control.

herbalist alternate therapist who prescribes herbs with a known medicinal effect.

herbal medicine prescientific medicine based on herbs; many effective drugs are the result of centuries of herbal medicine.

herbs by themselves, or in proper combination, herbs may enhance the body's normal healing process; not all herbs are necessarily safe or useful, simply because something is natural doesn't mean it's safe for human beings. At least 175,000 different species of flowering plants have been recorded.

Herceptin trastuzumab (Genentech): monoclonal antibody drug with limited success on breast cancer, now being tested for prostate cancer; initial test indicate that when combines with Taxol, caused tumor regression in mice; *under study.*

hereditary inherited from one's parents and earlier generations.

hereditary prostate cancer prostate cancer inherited from either the father's or mother's side of the family; considered hereditary if a patient's father and one or more brothers have had prostate cancer, or if three generations have had prostate cancer.

heredity historical distribution of biological characteristics through a group of related individuals via their DNA.

hesitancy difficulty in starting the flow of urine.

heterozygosity two different forms of the same gene in a cell.

hexasodium salt *see* **Suramin**.

Hgb *see* **hemoglobin**.

HGH human growth hormone.

HIFU *see* **high-intensity focused ultrasound**.

high-dose anti-androgen monotherapy anti-androgen is a compound, (usually a synthetic pharmaceutical), that blocks or otherwise interferes with the normal action of androgens at cellular receptor sites.

high dose ketoconazole (HDK) Nizoral, an anti-mycotic agent that inhibits or destroys fungal infections, produces a significant inhibition of the synthesis of androgens, estrogens and cortisol on prostate cancer patients; *under study*.

high dose rate (HDR) temporary implantation of radioactive iridium seeds in the prostate, followed by external beam radiation therapy; practiced in brachytherapy.

high-intensity focused ultrasound (HIFU) treatment for benign prostatic hyperplasia that uses heat from ultrasound energy to trim excess prostate tissue: *see* **ablatherm**.

histology study of the appearance and behavior of tissue, usually carried out under a microscope by a pathologist, (who is a physician), or a histologist, (who is not necessarily a physician).

hK2 *see* **human glandular kallikrein**.

HLA *see* **human leukocyte antigen**.

HLB Heitan-LaGarde-Bradford (American Biologics, Mexico): blood test for oxidating reactions.

HMEC-1 human microvascular cell.

holistic practice of treating the whole person, not simply the symptoms of the disease; the theory is that if a drug produces symptoms that are the same as the symptoms of a given disease, then a highly diluted form of the same drug will cure that disease: also known as **homeopathy**: *see* **University of Texas**.

homeopathy practice that asserts that the same agents or substances that cause a given illness can be used to treat it.

honvan tetrasodium phosphestrol (American Biologics, Mexico): synthetic hormone blocker.

hormonally independent cells cancer cells that are not affected by hormones.

hormone biologically active chemicals, some of which are responsible for the development of secondary sexual characteristics; hormones may be *endogenous* (produced by the endocrine glands), or *exogenou* (supplied from sources outside the body).

hormone blockade (HB) use of drugs or chemicals to interfere with the body's ability to produce the male androgen testosterone: *see* **ADT**, **CAB**, **CHB**, **CHT**.

hormone dependent prostate cancer prostate cancer that requires hormones from the body to grow and live; usually treated with HDT.

hormone deprivation therapy (HDT) therapy that tries to stop cancer cells from growing by depriving it of certain hormones.

hormone-independent prostate cancer prostate cancer that can grow without the presence of hormones; they will continue to grow whether or not the hormone supply is cut off; treatments such as radiation, surgery, or cyrosurgery are required to treat this type of cancer.

hormone receptor assay diagnostic test to determine whether cancer cells have receptor proteins for certain hormones; useful in treatments by hormonal therapy.

hormone refractory (HR) resistant or unresponsive to hormone therapy.

hormone therapy (HT) use of hormones, hormone analogs, and certain surgical techniques to treat disease, (e.g., advanced prostate cancer), either on their own or in combination with other hormones, or in combination with other methods of treatment. Because prostate cancer is usually dependent on male hormones to grow, hormonal therapy can be an effective means of alleviating symptoms and retarding the development of the disease.

horsetail *Equisetum arvense* herb used for flushing out bacterial and inflammatory diseases of the lower urinary tract: *see* **German Commission E**.

hospice place where terminally ill patients are cared for in an atmosphere that is as comfortable and pain-free as possible.

hot flash sudden sensation of warmth in the face, neck, and upper body; a side effect of many forms of hormone therapy.

hot spots images on a bone scan that may indicate sites of prostate cancer which has spread to the bones.

Hoxsey herbal treatment made up of (1) an externally used paste or powder, (2) a tonic taken orally; the internal herbs are adjusted on a case-by-case basis. Developed by Harry Hoxsey in the early 1940s and available in Mexico. Hoxsey died in 1974 from prostate cancer; *see* **University of Texas**.

HPC *see* **hereditary prostate cancer**.

HPC 1 (National Human Genome Research Institute): possible susceptibility for prostate cancer on chromosomes; may account for about 1 in 500 cases of prostate cancer; *under study*.

HPCX *see* **X chromosome**.

HPF high-powered field as seen with a microscope.

HR *see* **hormone refractory**.

HRPC hormone-refractory prostate cancer.

HRT hormone replacement therapy.

HSD *see* **hydroxysteroid dehydrogenase**.

HT *see* **hormone therapy**.

Htert (MIT, Harvard Medical School): chemical in a tumor cell that provides a template for the creation of telomerase; when altered to a negative form, blocks telomerase production; *under study*.

human genetic engineering *see* **gene therapy**.

Human genome project (HGP) international research project to find, identify, and decipher the structure of each of the 100,000 genes that occur in every cell; as of Sept. 1999, 70,000 genes have been deciphered and researchers know the function of about 10,000; *the balance are called* **orphan genes**.

human genome sciences six drug firms investigating genome databases.

human glandular kallikrein (hK2) new assay that may show the difference between cancer and benign disease; *under study.*

human leukocyte antigen (HLA) special markers found on white blood cells; HLA tissue typing is done to determine whether transplant recipient cells and potential donor cells are compatible.

HUVEC human umbilical vein endothelial cell.

Hybritech tandem PSA PSA test.

hydrazine sulfate seyhdrin a monoamine oxidase inhibitor and a common industrial chemical may act to stabilize tumors; claimed to cause tumor regression and subjective improvement in patients; proposed to treat progressive weight loss and the crippling characteristics of advanced cancer: *see* **University of Texas**.

hydrocortisone type of steroid normally but not exclusively produced by the adrenal glands; brand name is Cortef: *see* **cortisol hydrocortisone**.

hydrogenated, partially chemical process that adds hydrogen atoms to certain food oils to thicken them for use as a food.

hydroxysteroid dihydrotestosterone (HSD) enzyme that oxidizes or reduces testosterone to androstenedione, or vice versa.

hypercalcemia abnormally high concentrations of calcium in the blood, indicating leaching of calcium from bone; tumors raise serum calcium levels by destroying bone or by releasing PTH or a PTH-like substance, osteoclast-activating compound, prostaglandins, and perhaps, a vitamin D-like sterol. Symptoms of hypercalcemia may include drowsiness, lethargy, headaches, depression or apathy, irritability, confusion; weakness, muscle flaccidity, bone pain, pathologic fractures; signs of heart block, cardiac arrest in systole, hypertension; anorexia, nausea, vomiting, constipation, dehydration, polydipsia; renal polyuria, flank pain, and eventually, azotemia (excess of urea or other nitrogenous substances in the blood).

hyperimmune unusually rich in antibodies.

hyperoxygenation therapy proponents claim that cancer is caused by an oxygen deficiency and can be cured by exposing cells to more oxygen than they can tolerate; the most promoted agents are hydrogen peroxide, germanium sesquioxide, and ozone: *also known as* **bio-oxidative** and **oxidative therapy**.

hyperplasia enlargement of an organ or tissue because of an increase in the number of constituent cells: *see* **benign prostatic hyperplasia**.

hyper-reflexive bladder condition in which the patient has a strong urge to urinate, which can result in urine leakage.

hyperthermia treatment that uses heat; for example, heat produced by microwave radiation. In hyperthermia therapy, the body or selected areas are warmed for several hours to reduce PSA. First used in the 1970s as a cancer treatment; proponents claim that it changes the body's own tumor proteins into foreign proteins so that they can be recognized by the immune defense and defeated; also that it stops tumor growth immediately.

hypnosis therapy in which subject is placed in a state of intense concentration. Sometimes used for prostate cancer pain.

Hytrin terazosin (Abbott): drug that relaxes the prostate muscle and bladder neck to improve urine flow and help reduce bladder obstruction: *see* **alpha-1-adrenergic blockers**.

I

IAD intermittent androgen deprivation.

IADT intermittent androgen deprivation therapy.

I&D irrigation and drainage.

iatrogenic process adverse condition that results from the activity of, or treatment by, a physician or other health-care worker.

IAS *see* **intermittent androgen suppression**.

Ibandronate (Roche): three-month injection for the prevention and treatment of osteoporosis which may eliminate stomach upset.

IBM incident-based mortality.

Iceballs Internet mailing list for those interested in cryosurgery for prostate cancer.

ICHT *see* **intermittent combined hormone therapy**.

ICI intracavernosal injection.

ICTP type 1 carboxy-terminal telopeptide; a bone resorption marker.

Id1, Id3 (Memorial Sloan Kettering): two genes that play a vital role in the angiogenesis (forming of new blood vessels) process; *under study.*

IDE investigational device exemption.

IEUS image enhanced ultrasound screening; multi-colored displays indicating tumor density that correlates to Gleason categorizing; may be a replacement for biopsies; *under study.*

IFA immunofluorescent antibody.

IG immunoglobulin.

IGF insulin-like growth compound.

IGF-1 insulin-like growth compound-1; stimulates prostate cancer cell growth and osteoblast growth; men with a high level of this hormone have a four-fold risk of developing prostate cancer; *under study.*

IGFBP-2 insulin-like growth compound binding proteins (University Of Texas-Galveston): stimulates the growth of prostate cancer cells cultivated in tissue culture cells; may be possible to inhibit the action of IGFBP-2 with a specific antibody; *under study.*

IgG immunoglobulin G, a subclass of serum antibody produced in mammals.

IHT *see* **intermittent hormone therapy**.

IL-1 interleukin-1; may facilitate osteoblast (cell that forms bone) growth in addition to its other functions.

ILC *see* **interstitial laser coagulation**.

ILK (Kinetek Pharmaceuticals, Canada) growth factor protein that functions as a "master switch" in cell's communication network; turned off during cell development and growth; *under study.*

IM 862 (Cytran): nose drops that starve the lifelines of tumors while simultaneously building up the immune system to attack cancerous cells; may block production of angiogenesis growth compounds known as VEGF and bFGF; *under study.*

images anatomic pictures.

imaging technique or method allowing a physician to see something that would not normally be visible.

IMC-1C11 (ImClone Systems): anti-angiogenesis antibody that targets VEGFr by binding VEGF to its receptor; *under study.*

InjecTx an ethanol injection device; *see* **alcohol, absolute**.

IM-862 antiangiogenesis drug in clinical trials; *under study.*

ImmTher (Endorex): stimulates human monocytes to broad tumoricidal activity against a variety of human cancer cells; *under study.*

immune protected against a given infection or disease.

immune augmentative therapy (IAT) *see* **Govallo, Valentin I** and **Burton, Lawrence**; *see* **University of Texas**.

immune bodies antibodies that fight agents that are foreign in the body.

immune globulin blood protein fraction that contains antibodies.

immune serum serum that contains antibodies.

immune system biological system that protects a person or animal from the effects of foreign materials, such as bacteria, viruses, cancer cells, etc., which might cause sickness.

immunization process of protecting, by challenging from possible future infection, an individual immune system, with a weak and/or dead version of the infectious agent.

immunocytochemistry technique for staining cells, or tissue, using antibodies to identify an appropriate antigen.

immunology study of the body's mechanisms of developing resistance against disease or invasion by a foreign substance.

Immunology Research Foundation *see* **Burton, Lawrence**.

Immunology Researching Centre Ltd. *see* **Burton, Lawrence**.

immunoscintigraphy test to locate metastatic prostate cancer.

immunosuppressed having a lowered resistance to disease; may be due to a lowered white blood cell count resulting from radiation or chemotherapy.

immunotherapy treatments used to stimulate the body's immune system to mount an effective anti-immune attack against prostate cancer; theory is based on the principles of molecular biology, immunology, and genetics.

implant device that is inserted into the body; for example, a tiny container of radioactive material inserted in or near a tumor; also, a device to replace or substitute for an ability that has been lost; for example, a penile implant that can be surgically inserted into the penis to provide rigidity for intercourse.

impotence inability to have or to maintain an erection; may be the result of injury, radiation therapy, surgical resection of the prostate, hormonal deprivation therapy, or other aspects of neurological, vascular or disease processes: *see* **erectile dysfunction**.

IMRT *see* **intensity modulated radiation therapy**.

Incel biricodar dicitrat (Vertex): drug which may have activity against multidrug resistance in patients with advanced hormone-refractory prostate cancer; *under study*.

incision cut into the body or organ to allow access to the structure to be examined, repaired or removed.

incisional biopsy process in which a limited sample is obtained for evaluation without removing the entire mass, for example; in a needle aspiration, tissue is aspirated, or sucked from the suspected area.

incontinence loss of urinary control; there are various kinds and degrees of incontinence; see **overflow incontinence**, **stress incontinence** and **total incontinence**.

Incyte name used by eight drug firms combined to investigate genome databases.

IND investigational new drug.

indication reason for doing something or taking some action; also used to mean the approved clinical application of a pharmaceutical.

Indium 111 radioactive material injected into the patient taking a Prostascint scan; *see* **Prostascint**.

indole-3-carbinol (I3c) major constituent of cruciferous vegetables (broccoli, cabbage, and cauliflower), that has been shown to prevent cancer in animal models; being tested as a prostate cancer prevention drug; *under study*.

Indolplex brand name for an extract of cruciferous vegetables, containing dindolyl methane (DIM); may suppress the immune system and block side effects of hormonal blockade.

indurated excessive hardening or firmness of any body size; one of the signs of inflammation.

induration area of firmness or thickening.

indwelling catheter catheter that remains in the bladder.

infarct tissue death resulting from inadequate blood flow.

infection disease that results from microorganisms that invade the body, multiply, and cause injurious effects; there is no clear association between infection and prostate cancer.

infectious prostatitis inflammation of the prostate caused by bacteria.

infiltrating cancer cancer, that has grown from the site in which it originated, into the surrounding tissues.

inflammation reaction of tissue to injury: may be manifested by swelling, pain, or irritation of the injured area.

inflatable penile prosthesis (IPP) device surgically implanted in the penis that enables impotent men to have sexual intercourse.

informed consent permission to proceed in a prescribed manner, given by a patient, usually in writing, after being fully informed of the purposes and potential consequences of a medical, surgical procedure or treatment.

infusion technique for intravenously administration of drugs, or other treatments in liquid form, at a controlled rate.

infusion pump ambulatory device used to deliver a constant flow of medication; for example, to relieve pain.

inherited transmitted through genes from parents to offspring.

INK4a key tumor suppressor gene; *under study*.

inositol hexaniacinate variation of niacin; used for patients who need high doses of niacin.

in situ in place, localized, and confined to one area; a very early stage of non-invasive cancer.

Insulin (Bioplus Clinic, Mexico): claims that a state of profoundly lowered blood sugar kills cancer cells.

integrative medicine combination of Eastern, Western, and nonconventional medicine.

integrins a class of proteins on the surface of blood vessel cells that help in the integration of replicating endothelial cells into new blood vessels; under study: *see* **endothelial**.

Integrin alphavbeta3 antiangiogenesis drug; *under study: see* **integrins**.

intensity modulated radiation therapy (IMRT) sophisticated computer program that pinpoints the cancer for radiation treatment so that the surrounding healthy tissue of the bladder and rectum is spared.

interferon body protein that affects antibody production and can regulate the immune system.

interferon alfa substance produced by peripheral blood leukocytes when exposed to live or inactivated virus, double-stranded RNA, or bacterial products; causes activation of natural-killer cells.

interferon alfa–2a substance consisting of 165 amino acid residues; used extensively as an antitumor agent.

interleukin any one of several compounds produced by white blood cells that function in regulating the immune system.

interleukin-12 (IL-12) antiangiogenesis drug in clinical trials; *under study*.

intermittent androgen suppression (IAS) pause in hormone therapy.

intermittent combined hormone therapy (ICHT) hormonal treatment with LHRH agonists and an antiandrogen that is administered intermittently.

intermittent hormone therapy (IHT) hormone therapy administered with periods of cessation or inactivity.

internal radiation therapy *see* **brachytherapy** and **radiation therapy**.

International Health Institute *see* **Kelley, William**.

International prostate symptom score (IPSS) score based on answers to seven questions concerning urinary symptoms, with each question assigned points from 0 to 5, indicating increasing severity of the indicated symptom.

international unit (IU) unit in an international system that standardizes measures of weight and volume.

Interstim continence control therapy (Medtronic): a treatment for urinary urge incontinence by electrical stimulation of the nerves in the lower region of the spine.

interstitial within a particular organ.

interstitial laser coagulation (ILC) laser surgery; the surgeon inserts a scopelike device through the penis to the prostate area; a fiber optic then destroys a precise area of the enlarged gland; the destroyed tissue is absorbed naturally by the body.

interstitial radiation therapy radiation treatment of the prostate using radioactive pellets or seeds; *see* **brachytherapy**.

Intimex brand name product, containing various herbs in lipsomes; used for sexual dysfunction.

intramuscular (I.M.) administration of a medication by needle injection into a muscle of the body, usually in the upper arm or thigh.

intraoperative radiotherapy radiation therapy given in the operating room when vital organs overlie the area of the tumor; during the operation, the surgeon temporarily moves the normal organs out of the way so radiation can be applied directly to the tumor.

intravenous (IV) through a vein.

intravenous pyelogram (IVP) procedure in which an X-ray absorbing dye is introduced into the urinary tract for contrast in order to allow the physician to visualize the tract during an X-ray examination; used to check for the spread of cancer to the kidneys and bladder.

intravenous urography test to study bladder outflow problems.

invasive requiring an incision or the insertion of an instrument or substance into the body.

invasive cancer cancer that has spread beyond its site of origin into the surrounding tissues.

investigational drugs which are allowed by the FDA for use in clinical trials, but not approved for sale to the general public.

in vitro within a test tube or other container outside a living organism.

in vivo within a body; human or animal.

involution changes in organic functioning in any aging organ, such as the prostate.

Iodine-125 radioactive isotope implanted into the gland and used in brachytherapy.

IP Iprifavone synthetic soy derivative; may inhibit bone loss and decrease pain associated with osteoporosis.

IP-6 inositol hexaphosphate, compound extracted from soybeans and the bran portion of brown rice; may decrease the blood's tendency to clot; *under study.*

I-plant (Implant Sciences): approved by the FDA as a radioactive seed implant with non-radioactive xenon-124 gas; a nuclear reactor transmutes the xenon-124 into iodine-125, which is embedded beneath the surface of the core; permits the inventorying of seed cores in large quantity until used.

IPP *see* **inflatable penile prosthesis**.

ipriflavone (IP) organic derivative of isoflavone with a chemical structure in plants similar to estrogen; may inhibit bone loss and decrease pain associated with osteoporosis.

Iressa ZD1839 (Astra/Zeneca): part of a drug class called signal transduction inhibitors; stops signals within tumor cells, resulting in cessation of the proliferation process; *under study.*

Iridium-192 radioactive isotope, with a prolonged half-life, used in brachytherapy seed implant.

iridology alternate therapy based on the theory that disease can be detected by examining the iris of the eye.

iron part of the blood-chemistry panel test: indicates whether iron is present in the sample; low results may be associated with anemic states.

irritated prostate prostate condition characterized by discomfort or pain.

isatis indigotica Chinese herb, one of eight in the herbal formula *PC SPES;* contains beta-sitosterol; oral beta-sitosterol is said to reduce cancer growth in animal studies.

iscador extract of mistletoe proposed for the treatment of cancer in 1920 by Rudolph Steiner, who founded the Society for Cancer Research for the practice of anthroposophical medicine; a 1962 report by the society stated that the time of harvesting of the plants is important because they react to the influence of the sun, moon, and planets.

ischuria retention of urine.

ISIS 3521 (Isis/Novartis): antisense, anticancer compound that is an inhibitor of protein kinase C-alpha expression; may inhibit gene transfers from one generation to another; *under study.*

isoflavone genistein constituent in soy; genistein is one of the isoflavones in soy; may act as weak estrogens and leave less room for strong ones; may reduce the risk of hormone dependent cancer.

isoprenoids plant compounds that may suppress an enzyme that normally allows cancer cells to grow and split; lycopene, e.g, found in tomatoes, is an isoprenoid.

itch *see* **pruritus**.

ITT indigo diode laser thermotherapy for transurethral resection of the prostate (TURP); *under study*: *see* TURP.

IU *see* **international unit**.

IV *see* **intravenous**.

IVP *see* **intravenous pyelogram**.

J

jaundice yellowish skin color; usually indicating damage to the liver.

java tea *Orthosiohonis folium* irrigation therapy for inflammatory diseases of the lower urinary tract: *see* **German Commission E**.

junk DNA dead genes, failed genes and viral genes.

K

K symbol for potassium.

kahalide F (Pharma Mar/Zeltia, Spain): extract from a Hawaiian marine mollusk found effective in animal trials on prostate cancer; *under study*.

Kegel exercises set of exercises designed to improve the strength of the muscles used in urinating; these are done by squeezing and tightening the buttocks; practiced while standing to urinate or at other times.

Keller, Helmut Dr. chief of the Klinik Winnerhof, Bad Wiessee, Germany.

Kelley, William D., D.D.S. founded of the International Health Institute in the 1960s; according to some patients, Kelley examined the patient's blood and then prescribed a diet, dietary supplements, and enzymes; later, his technicians used a 3,200-item patient questionnaire and provided a lengthy computer printout covering foods, supplements, lifestyle changes, etc.

ketoconazole *see* **Nizoral**.

kidney one of a pair of organs, whose primary function is to filter the circulating blood, selectively retaining portions of the blood and removing waste material; the kidneys are connected by the ureters to the bladder.

kidney bean pods *Phaseoli fructus sine semine* pods, without seeds, a supportive treatment for inability to urinate: ***see*** **German Commission E**.

kinases molecules needed for the cell to progress through its life cycle.

Klinik Winnerhof offers alternative oncological medicine, hyperthermia; located in Bad Wiessee, Germany.

krestin *see* **coriolus versicolor**.

Kytril granisetron hydrochloride (SmithKline Beecham): drug used to prevent nausea and vomiting associated with chemotherapy.

L

laetrile *see* **vitamin B-17**.

laparoscope viewing tube that enables a physician to look directly at an investigative area.

laparoscopic lymphadenectomy using a laparoscope, the removal of pelvic lymph nodes through four small incisions in the lower abdominal region.

laparoscopic lymph node dissection use of a laparoscope to remove lymph nodes to test for cancer.

laparoscopy technique that allows a physician to observe internal organs through optical equipment inserted into the body through a small surgical incision.

laser (light amplification by stimulated emission of radiation) very high-intensity light source used to remove tissue, avoiding surgical procedures.

latent insignificant or irrelevant; for example, latent prostate cancer; also known as *incidental prostate cancer;* a form of prostate cancer that is of no clinical significance to the patient when it is discovered.

lateral-lobe enlargement type of BPH in which the prostate tissue squeezes the pectoral enlargement of the urethra; can cause urinary problems.

LBA live blood analysis (American Biologics, Mexico): laboratory test to examine living blood compounds for white and red cells of the blood-chemistry panel test: a group of five enzymes found in most bodily tissues, and like all enzymes, serves to catalyze other biochemical reactions; elevated values can indicate kidney or heart problems.

LDL cholesterol low-density lipoprotein, part of the blood-chemistry panel test: referred to as the "bad" part of cholesterol, transports cholesterol and deposits it on the walls of the arteries; the lower the LDL cholesterol concentration, the lower the risk of cardiovascular disease.

LE local excision.

lead time bias survival advantage of patients whose cancers are diagnosed early as part of a screening program.

LED, LEP (NeoPharm): offshoots of two common cancer drugs, Doxorubicin and Taxol; directed to the evaluation of the reduction of side effects, thus enabling patients to tolerate higher drug doses; *under study.*

LEF life extension foundation; originally organized to help in the aging process, now gives information on prostate cancer, among other diseases.

length time bias the difference between screened and clinical patients; screening may indicate an early cancer, while a clinical patient may indicate a more advanced cancer.

lentinan (Ajinomoto, Japan): purified extract of shiitake mushroom that may activate T-cells and macrophages (immune cells) that destroy and ingest invading microorganisms; licensed in Japan for cancer treatment; *under study.*

leukocytes white blood cells that circulate in the blood; are responsible for protective functions, such as immunological.

leuprolide acetate *see* **Lupron**.

Leuvectin (Vical): drug may be effective in causing a targeted immune response against prostate cancer cells; *under study.*

levels of evidence term used by the U.S. public health community to categorize various diseases: A level means that there are randomized control and other data to support it; B level means that there are cases of controlled studies; C level means that there have been some individual series where there has been a change in apparent disease stage; and D level means that there is very little evidence to support it: prostate cancer is classified by the U.S. Preventive Task Force, in the D level category of evidence.

LF laser fulguration.

LFT liver function test.

LH luteinizing hormone; a hormone produced in the pituitary gland that promotes secretion of male and female sex hormones.

LH-FSH luteinizing hormone-follicle-stimulating hormone.

LH-RF luteinizing hormone releasing compound.

LHRH *see* **luteinizing hormone-releasing hormone**.

LHRH agonist compound that is similar to LHRH; luteinizing hormone is produced in the pituitary gland; stimulates the testes to produce testosterone; the LHRH is one step up the chemical chain, in that it is a hormone that stimulates production of LH. An agonist compound is a drug that works like LHRH; however, this chemically similar agent supersedes the body's normal LHRH, with the result that the LH never gets the opportunity to stimulate the production of testosterone; the LHRH agonists are used commonly to treat prostate cancer by eliminating the testosterone needed to stimulate the reproduction of cancer cells; LHRH agonists are used in the palliative hormonal treatment of advanced prostate cancer and sometimes in the adjuvant and neoadjuvant hormonal treatment of earlier stages of prostate cancer.

Liarozole experimental drug hoped to lower PSA; withdrawn from clinical trials Dec. 7, 1998.

Liazal (Janssen): drug that is a differentiating agent affecting hormone dependent and independent cells; *under study.*

libido interest in sexual activity; sex drive.

licochalone (Robert Johnson Medical School): compound, found in licorice root; may increase tumor sensitivity to anticancer agents; the extract may act as a phytoestrogen, a plant version of the hormone estrogen, known to be involved in several types of cancers; *under study.*

licoflavone putresin; compound known to bind to cholesterol.

licorice root the active component, glycyrrhizin acid, is found only in naturally flavored black licorice; may protect against prostate cancer by preventing formation of testosterone.

lifestyle and disease prevention theories and practices designed to prevent the development of illness, identify and treat risk factors, and support the healing and recovery process.

lifestyle therapy lifestyle management that includes behavioral or dietary changes, exercise, stress management and addiction control.

ligand (Synergene Therapeutics): compound which can recognize and attach to the chemical doorways on the surface of cells; tested to carry liposomes and p53 genes directly to tumor cells.

limonene an oil found in skin of citrus fruits, claimed to curtail tumor growth.

linear accelerator machine that produces high-energy photon or neutron particles directed to destroy cancer cells.

linkage analysis gene-hunting technique that traces patterns of heredity in high-risk families.

linoleic acid an essential fatty acid; used in the synthesis of other essential fatty acids; a polyunsaturate that can be obtained from dietary sources such as seeds, oils, vegetables, and grains; a deficiency can produce a form of dermatitis.

Linimide roquinimex (SUNY StonyBrook/Pharmacia & Upjohn): drug that may shrink prostate tumors through a process of anti-angiogenesis.

lipemic blood blood sample with a high proportion of fatty products.

lipids biological molecules soluble in apolar solvents: *see* **apolar**.

lipsome synthetic bilayer lipid membrane-bound vesicle formed by emulsification of cell membranes; used for drug delivery.

live cell therapy injection of whole tissue compounds from an animal fetus; *under study.*

liver scan examination of the liver, in which a trace dose of a radioactive substance is injected into the blood, making it possible to visualize the organ via X-ray.

Living Foundation Medical Center *see* **Livingston-Wheeler, Virginia**.

Livingston-Wheeler, Virginia opened the Living Foundation Medical Center in San Diego in 1969; treatment includes a wide multiple approach to cancer, ranging from antibiotics to psychosocial intervention to enemas, along with a vegetarian whole-foods diet; more than 10,000 patients have been treated since the clinic opened, but no survival data is stated.

LN *see* **lymph nodes**: the notation 1/3 LN, indicates that 1 of 3 lymph nodes excised at surgery had metastatic disease.

LNCap laboratory tumor model built from prostate cancer tumor; removed from affected lymph nodes.

lobe one of two or more segments or anatomical portions of an organ, as in the prostate, lung, thyroid, brain, etc.

localized restricted to a well-defined area.

locally advanced prostate cancer advanced beyond the immediate area of the prostate; there are several categories; *see* **unilateral extracapsular extension, bilateral extracapsular extension, seminal vesicles**, and **lymph nodes**.

Lodine XL drug that interferes with COX-2 activity; COX-2 causes rapid proliferation of cell division in cancer cells; Lodine XL is an arthritis drug, that when combined with Mevacor (*lovastatin*), increases its cancer-cell kill rate; *under study*: *see* **COX-2, Lovastatin**.

lovage root *Levisticum officinalis* perennial herb; irrigation therapy for inflammation of the lower urinary tract: *see* **German Commission E.**

Lovastatin nonsteroidal anti-inflammatory drug; in high dosage may reduce tumor growth; *under study*: *see* **NSAID**.

lower back pain regional pain which may be due to a prostate disorder since veins from the prostate drain blood into this region.

LSESr lipo-sterolic extract of saw palmetto.

Lupron *leuprolide acetate* (TAP Holdings): a long-acting LHRH analog, injected monthly and used in chemical castration and combination hormonal therapy; a longer-acting depot injection, effective over three months, is also available.

luteinizing hormone releasing hormone (LH-Rh or LHRH) hormone responsible for stimulating the production of testosterone in the body: *see* LHRH agonist.

LUTS lower urinary tract symptoms, a symptom of BPH: *see* **benign prostatic hyperplasia**.

lycopene antioxidant; responsible for the red coloring of tomatoes, raspberries, and watermelon; laboratory studies have shown it to have a beneficial effect against prostate cancer.

lymph clear fluid in which all of the cells in the body are constantly bathed; carries cells that help fight infection.

lymphadenectomy pelvic lymph node dissection, a procedure which involves the removal and microscopic examination of selected lymph nodes, a common site of metastatic disease with prostate cancer; this procedure may be performed prior to the removal of the prostate gland; an incisional biopsy (laparoscopic lymphadenectomy) may also be performed.

lymphangiogram X-ray that makes use of a contrast agent to visualize lymph nodes and organs to determine whether cancer has spread to them.

lymphatic system tissues and organs that produce, store, and carry cells as well as secretions that fight infection; includes bone marrow, spleen, thymus, lymph nodes, and channels that carry lymph fluid.

lymph node involvement presence of tumor cells in the lymph nodes of the pelvis.

lymph nodes (LN) small rounded tissue structures that occur throughout the body, which filter the clear fluid known as lymph or lymphatic fluid; lymph nodes filter out bacteria and other organisms, as well as cancer cells; when prostate cancer is found in the pelvic lymph nodes, the patient has locally advanced prostate cancer.

lymphocyte white blood cell that fights bacterial and viral infections: *see* **B-cell** and **T-cell**.

lymphokine substance produced by the immune system, claimed to be a biological therapy against cancer.

lymphoma malignancy of the lymphoid tissue.

lyprinol New Zealand green-lipped mussel extract that is claimed to kill cancer cells in a laboratory situation; *under study*.

lytic lesions as seen on X-rays, rarefied areas of bone, sites of destruction by cancer cells; lesions appear black on affected bone images.

M

M0, M1 *see* **staging, tumor or cancer**.

MAb monoclonal antibody with the ability to specifically target tumor sites while sparing normal tissues.

MAB maximal androgen blockade: *see* **combined hormone therapy**.

macrobiotic diet from **macros** (long) and **bios** (life); diet in which 50 to 60 percent of food intake is from whole cereals and grains; rest from vegetables, beans, fermented soy products, sea vegetables, teas and soups from appropriate ingredients; small amounts of white-meat fish and fresh organic fruits can be included.

macrophage immune cell, mostly in solid tissues, that ingests and destroys invading microorganisms.

MAD maximal androgen deprivation: *see* **combined hormone therapy.**

magnetic resonance absorption of specific frequencies of radio and microwave radiation by atoms placed in a strong magnetic field.

magnetic resonance imaging (MRI) imaging process that uses magnetic resonance with atoms in body tissues to produce distinct cross-sectional, and three-dimensional images of internal organs; MRI is of use in staging biopsy-proven prostate cancer.

magnetic resonance spectroscope imaging (MRSI) imaging using a magnetic field and radio waves to obtain pictures based on the concentration of cellular chemicals; detects cellular metabolites, citrate, creatine, and choline.

malignancy growth or tumor composed of cancerous cells.

malignant cancerous; tending to become progressively worse and to result in death; having the invasive and metastatic properties of cancer.

malignin *see* **peptides**.

manipulative systems based on manipulation and/or movement of the body such as chiropractic medicine, massage, and unconventional physical therapies.

Manner, Harold *see* **metabolic therapy**.

mannitol sugar that opens the blood-brain barrier and tends to concentrate carnivora in the brain; *see* **carnivora**.

margin, surgical outer edge of the tissue removed during surgery; if the surgical margin of the biopsy shows no sign of cancer, "negative margins," the prognosis is favorable.

marijuana *Cannabis sativa* herb used for palliation of painful urinary-tract disorders.

marijuana patch (Albany College of Pharmacy/ACS): delivers controlled doses to ease pain; *under study.*

Marimastat (British Biotech): drug, taken orally, that may inhibit blood flow to tumors, thus blocking further growth; *under study.*

marker indication of malignant potential for prostate cancer.

Maxamine (Maxim): drug, when used in combination with cytokines, will boost immune function; *under study.*

mcg/l micrograms per liter; 1,000 micrograms equal 1 gram.

MCH mean cell hemoglobin, a measure of the amount of hemoglobin within each red cell; part of the complete blood-count.

McmJ protein needed for cell growth that notifies DNA to replicate itself; found in high concentrations in many cancers; *under study.*

MCV mean cell volume, a measure of the average size of the red blood cells; part of the complete blood-count.

M.D. medical doctor.

MDR multiple drug resistance, genetic technique to protect bone marrow from the toxic effects of cancer chemotherapy; *under study.*

MDX-210 (Medarex): biospecific antibody that targets HER-2, a protein found in excess on the surface of certain cancer cells; *under study.*

mean platelet volume measure of platelet size; may help the doctor evaluate blood platelet counts, a measure of effective blood clotting: *see* **platelet**.

medical castration hormonal therapy using drugs instead of surgery to inhibit testosterone production by the testes.

medical oncologist physician specializing in the use of medicines (rather than surgery) to treat cancer.

medical radiation physicist individual who ensures that radiation equipment is working properly by taking precise measurements of the radiation beam characteristics; also mapping of area to be treated with shielding of vital structures: *see* **dosimetrist**.

meds medicines.

Megace megestrol acetate (Bristol-Myers Squibb): drug that can reduce hot flashes caused by hormonal treatment side effects.

megestrol acetate *see* **Megace**.

melacine melanoma vaccine being tested for prostate cancer; *under study.*

melatonin hormone present in plant and animal life form, has been used to assist the immune system in fighting viruses and bacterial infections, acts as an aid to sleep, enhances libido and protects against DNA damage: *see* **University of Texas**.

membranes thin structure separating the inside of a cell from the outside; able to constantly adapt to change from environmental conditions.

messenger RNA transcripts of DNA sequences used to make proteins.

meta-analysis statistical technique that permits an overview of all studies concerning a certain issue.

metabolic therapy based on the theory that degenerative disease is the result of metabolic imbalance caused by a buildup of toxic substances in the body; treatment consists of a natural food diet, coffee enemas, vitamins, minerals, glandulars, enzymes, laetrile, etc. A clinic founded by Harold Manner, Ph.D., still operates in Mexico.

metalloproteinases protein with a metal ion bound to it.

metastasis (mets) secondary tumor formed as a result of cancer cells from a primary tumor site, e.g., the prostate, traveling through the body to a new site and then growing there; plural, *metastases.*

metastasis, local spread of prostate tumor into regional lymph nodes and/or the adjacent seminal vesicles.

metastasize to spread to other parts of the body.

Metastat antiangiogenesis drug; *under study.*

metastatic having the characteristics of a secondary tumor.

metastatic cancer cancer that has spread to a site distant from the original site.

metastatic work up group of tests, including bone scans, X-rays, and blood tests; to ascertain whether a cancer has metastasized to distant locations.

Metastron strontium 89 (Sr89) (Amersham): injectable non-narcotic radioactive medication; used to relieve bone pain in patients with prostate cancer who no longer respond to hormones or chemotherapy.

metenkephalin *Methionine enkephalin* natural endorphin produced in the brain.

meters squared measurement term for calculating body surface area; used for chemotherapy.

meth-1, meth-2 (UCLA/Human Genome Sciences): two human proteins that inhibit the formation of new blood vessels; may inhibit cancer through suppression of blood supply to tumor sites; *under study.*

Methadone plus epidural anesthesia given to men undergoing prostate surgery.

mets *see* **metastasis**.

mg/dl milligrams per deciliter; unit of concentration in the blood, now preferred over mg/ml.

MGI 114 (Pharmacia & Upjohn): derived from a mushroom; shows antitumor activity in patients with hormone refractory prostate cancer; *under study*: *see* **acylfulvenes**.

mgn-3 (Daiwa): manufacturer claims this natural supplement may be an immune system builder.

Miacalcin calcitonin-salmon (Sandoz): drug administrated by injection, used to prevent and treat osteoporosis in women.

microbe microscopic organism.

micrometastases metastases that may not be detected because of their small size.

microwave radiation *see* **hyperthermia**.

micturition urination.

middle lobe enlargement form of benign prostatic hyperplasia in which the prostate gland grows into the bladder and can partially or totally block the flow of urine from the bladder into the urethra.

milk thistle *Silybum marianum* antioxidant herb that may protect the liver cells: *see* **German Commission E**.

Millennium five drug firms combined to investigate cancer genes.

MIMiC a binary intensity modulating collimator.

mind-body medicine involves behavioral psychological, social and spiritual approaches to health; a sub-category is the mind-body systems; when used in combination with lifestyle interventions; can be a part of a traditional medical system.

mineral natural occurring element found in the earth that is also present in the body, allows the performance of necessary functions; there are two basic groups of minerals: (1) macro, such as calcium, magnesium, potassium, and sodium, and (2) trace, such as iodine, iron, selenium, and zinc.

mini-laparotomy examination with a laparoscope of pelvic and other lymph nodes via a small incision to determine if they are cancerous.

minimum daily requirements (MDR) minimum amount of a substance that must be ingested to prevent dietary deficiency.

misstaging assignment of an incorrect clinical stage at the time of initial diagnosis.

mistletoe *Viscum album* herb used to stimulate the immune system and to kill cancer cells: *see* **German Commission E, University of Texas**.

mitosis process of cell division; the number of mitoses indicates the number of tumor cells replicating.

mitoxantrone *see* **Novantrone**.

MMAC1 *see* **pten.**

mmol/l millimole per liter (1/1,000 concentration) this is the normal expression for a substance found to be in body cells or solutions, rather than in mole per liter (m/l).

mmp matrix metalloproteinase enzyme; may play a pivotal role in tumor cell invasion and angiogenesis; *under study*.

modality type of therapy, such as chemotherapy, surgery, or radiotherapy.

modified citrus pectin compound derived from citrus fruits where the pH and polysaccharides have been altered to form groups of the simple sugar galactose; may block or inhibit the binding of cancer cells to other normal cells in rats; also being evaluated as an antiangiogenic agent: *see* **University of Texas**.

modulation cell's ability to adapt to an environment.

monoclonal formed from a single group of identical cells.

monoclonal antibody laboratory-produced version of a natural antibody that our immune system produces to fight diseases: *see* **Prostascint**.

monoclonal therapy antibody-based therapy; *under study*.

monocytes type of blood cell that is present in chronic infections; part of the blood count.

monotherapy one-chemical suppression treatment used to reduce testosterone to castration levels; also called HT, or hormone therapy: *see* **androgen deprivation therapy, combined hormone therapy**.

Monurol fosfomycin trometamol (Forest): drug used to treat uncomplicated urinary tract infection.

morbidity unhealthy consequences and complications resulting from treatment; also, disease rate in a given population.

morphological related to, or concerned with, form or structure; used to describe cancer or tumor cells.

mortality death rate resulting from a certain procedure, type of cancer, etc.

mouse model mouse used in laboratory experiments because it has specific characteristics that resemble human disease or disorder.

MRI *see* **magnetic resonance imaging**.

MRS magnetic resonance spectroscope.

MRSI *see* **magnetic resonance spectroscope imaging**.

MSS mean system score.

MTD maximum tolerated dose.

MTH-68 *see* **Csatary, Laszlo**.

MuJ 591 monoclonal antibody drug used in treating hormone refractory patients; *under study*.

multi-leaf collimator (MLC) shields the radiation beam to match the anatomy of the prostate.

multimodal approach varied approach to dealing with prostate cancer including diet and exercise.

mu opiate (John Hopkins University): gene that may be responsible for the molecule that binds with the body's own painkilling chemicals; bonds with peptides, if many peptides are present, the perception of pain is diminished; *under study.*

musculature muscular apparatus of the body or any part of it.

Muse alprostadil (Vivus): suppository injected into the urethra for erectile dysfunction.

mutagenicity production of genetic alterations.

mutation sudden change in an inherited characteristic; mutations of androgen-receptor genes have been found in patients with metastatic androgen-independent, (refractory), prostate cancer; two of these receptors could be activated by progesterone and estrogen, indicating that such mutations could be a reason why prostate cancer becomes refractory.

M-Vax world's first cancer vaccine designed to fight malignant melanoma; made from patient's own melanoma cells that have been modified to permit the body's immune system to identify them; vaccines for additional cancers are being developed; *under study.*

Mx notation indicating that metastases can not be or have not been evaluated.

myelosuppression decrease in the capacity of bone marrow to produce cells released in the blood; increases susceptibility to infection and produces fatigue in a patient undergoing treatment.

Myriad name used by four drug firm combination to investigate prostate cancer genes.

N

N0-N3 *see* **staging, tumor or cancer**.

nadir the lowest point reached; for example, in a series of PSA values.

naltrexone *see* **Revia**.

nanotechnology (Rice University): building things one atom at a time; manipulate cells at the molecular level and produce self-replicating matter; concept is to manipulate atoms individually and place them to produce the expected result; devices powered by nanocomputers will search, seek out, and destroy cancer cells in the body; *under study.*

National prostatic cancer project (NPCP) randomized trials in prostate cancer treatment; found survival differences between chemotherapy and standard therapy were negligible.

natural killer cells (NK) white blood cells that attack viruses and cancer cells.

naturopathy medicine an approach to health care based on the theory that the body and mind have the ability to restore and maintain health; first used in 1892, naturopathy flourished during the early part of the 20th century; declined during the 1940s and 1950s, but is becoming popular again as health-conscious people look for alternatives to traditional health care. A naturopathic physician should be licensed as a doctor of naturopathic medicine in those states that grant licenses.

N.D. naturopathic doctor; emphasizes healing power of nature and the importance of determining and removing the underlying cause of disease.

NDA new drug application.

NDPSA nondetectable PSA.

nd:yag (Trimedyne): laser treatment for benign prostatic hyperplasia; *under study.*

necrosis the sum of the morphological (structure of animals and plants) changes indicative of cell death and caused by the progressive degradative action of enzymes; may affect groups of cells or part of a structure or an organ: *see* **apoptosis**.

NED no evidence of disease.

negative (Neg) may indicate absence (qualitative meaning) or presence, but not in clinically significant amount (quantitative meaning), that does not show the presence of the substance or material for which the test was carried out; for example, a negative bone scan would show no sign of apparent bone metastases; both an implied qualitative and quantitative assessment.

neoadjuvant added before; for example, neoadjuvant hormone therapy is given prior to another form of treatment, such as a radical prostatectomy.

neoplasia usually refers to new growth; the same as tumor, which may be benign or malignant.

neoplasm abnormal growth that is often used to describe a cancer; may be benign or malignant.

neovastat AE-941 angiogensis inhibitor, derived from shark cartilage, that may prevent the formation of new blood vessels; inhibiting cancer growth.

NER nucleotide excision repair; a variety of proteins necessary to detect and repair injuries from ultraviolet radiation, X-rays, and chemical toxins.

nerve blocks anesthesia that is injected at a certain point on a nerve, blocking sensation over an expected area of sensation.

nerve root clipping cutting the nerves, which are responsible for carrying pain sensations; a method to control pain.

nerve-sparing surgery prostatectomy procedure preserving the nerves that affect sexual and related functions.

nervous bladder condition characterized by a tendency to urinate in response to emotional stress.

Neupogen filgrastim (Amgen): drug used to decrease the incidence of infection; treatment for slow white blood cell recovery following chemotherapy.

neuroendocrine cell specialized neurons which secrete hormones.

neuron-specific enolase (NSE) a specific marker for tumors that express proteins or enzymes reflective of de-differentiated tumor cell populations, such as small cell prostate cancer; when both the CgA and the NSE are elevated, the prognosis is considered poor.

neurons, spinal cord (Memorial Sloan-Kettering): responsible for chronic pain and may be controlled by a drug; *under study.*

neurovascular both the neurologic and vascular structures: *see* **vascular**.

neurovascular bundle two groups of nerves and blood vessels, located on each side of the prostate, that aid in achieving an erection; if one or both of these groups are spared during surgery, normal erections may be experienced by a patient.

neutron beam radiation use of neutron, an atomic particle, to treat cancer.

neutron particles supplement to photon beams of radiation to help improve the effectiveness of the therapy.

neutrophil white blood cell types in the circulating blood; responsible for fighting infections.

ng/ml nanograms per milliliter, a unit of concentration used in the evaluation of many biological constituents; the expression of the results of a PSA test; a PSA level of 5 indicates 5 ng/ml.

NHB neoadjuvant hormone blockade.

NHT neoadjuvant hormone therapy.

niacinamide a form of vitamin B3; may be helpful with osteoarthritis.

NIDDK (NCI) group studying basic and clinical investigations of prostate disorders.

NIEHS, NHGRI NCI programs to identify genetic changes in the cell which lead to the initiation and progression of prostate cancer.

Nilandron nilutamide (Hoechst Marion Roussel): a nonsteroidal antiandrogen, used as add-on therapy following surgical or chemical castration due to prostate cancer; reduces bone pain in men with advanced prostate cancer: known in Canada as Anandron.

Nilutamide *See* **Anandron, Nilandron**.

NIMH NCI program to study the effects of stress and emotion in men with prostate cancer.

NINR NIC program in research on symptom management following prostate cancer surgery.

Nizoral ketoconazole (Janssen): high doses, drug administered to shut down the adrenal gland cortex, eliminating its production of testosterone; used with an LHRH agonist, (e.g., Lupron), to eliminate essentially all testosterone when combined hormone therapy fails.

NK-cell assay test to verify that circulating tumor cells, which have metastasized, are not mistaken for leukemia.

NK cells natural killer cells; NK cells can kill tumor cells.

NL nil; non-detectable response.

NMP nuclear matrix proteins; a highly insoluble filamentous network that is believed to play a role in maintaining nuclear architecture and organizing nuclear metabolism.

NMP 22 (Matritech): test for urinary bladder cancer; being modified for prostate and breast cancers; test is based on the level of NMPs detected in body fluids and correlated with the presence of early stage cancerous abnormalities.

NMR nuclear magnetic resonance.

nocturia the need to urinate frequently at night.

node-positive disease cancer that has invaded the lymph nodes; classified as "advanced" or "systemic." In the older Jewett-Whitmore staging system, it was classified as stage D1 disease.

nodule a small, circumscribed mass.

Nolvadex *see* **tamoxifen**.

nonbacterial prostatitis inflammation of the prostate, not due to a specific (identifiable) bacteria.

noninfectious prostatitis inflammation of the prostate in which no infectious agent is detected by laboratory analysis.

noninvasive examination or treatment procedure that does not require an incision, or insertion of an instrument, or substance into the body; such as an ultrasound examination.

norman couture incontinence device with a specially designed brief, consisting of tubes and bag constructed to provide patient comfort.

Novantrone mitoxantrone (Immunex/Lederle): drug used to treat hormone-resistant prostate cancer; *under study* as an antineoplaston which seems to interfere with the growth of cancer cells; being tested with Prednisone to reduce pain: *see* **AG 3340**.

NPT nonproven therapy.

ns-49 (Abbott): urinary stress incontinence; *under study*.

NSAID nonsteroidal anti-inflammatory drug; a large group of anti-inflammatory agents that work by inhibiting the production of prostaglandins.

NSE *see* **neuron-specific enolase**.

NTG nitroglycerin.

nuclear medicine specialty in medicine utilizing nuclear science; area of the hospital where bone scans and other medical treatments using nuclear science are conducted.

nuclear scan method that uses a weak radioactive material injected into the bloodstream and taken up by the body; an X-ray-type machine scans the body while taking pictures for diagnostic evaluation.

nuclear weapons exposure to radiation and chemicals in the production of nuclear weapons may produce cancer; prostate cancer is mentioned.

nucleus concentrated portion of a cell that houses the chromosomes.

nutrition series of processes by which an organism takes in and assimilates food for promoting growth and replacing worn out or injured tissues. The University of Texas, Anderson Cancer Center guidelines for the prevention and limitation of prostate cancer are: limit fat, (20% of energy intake); fruits and vegetables, (5 daily); fiber, (25-35 g); vitamin E, (800 IU); vitamin C, (500 mg), and soy protein, (40–60 g).

nv-06 (Monash Institute/Novogen, Australia): synthetic version of a naturally occurring compound found in human tissues, known as phenolic hormones; may reverse the cancer process once it is underway; *under study.*

Nx nodes, (lymph), cannot be, or have not been, microscopically evaluated for metastatic tumor.

O

OCT *see* **oral chelation therapy**.

off-label use of a prescription drug for a disease not recommended or tested by the FDA.

Oltipraz (Memorial Sloan-Kettering): prostate cancer prevention drug; *under study.*

OLX-514 antiangiogenesis drug; *under study.*

omega-3 polyunsaturated fat; may protect the prostate; found in cold-water fish such as herring, mackerel, salmon and tuna; *under study*: *see* **essential fatty acids**.

oncogene a gene that normally plays a role in the growth of cells, but when mutated, can cause the transformation of normal cells into cancer cells.

oncogenic tumor causing.

oncologist physician who specializes in the treatment of various types of cancer.

oncology branch of medical science dealing with tumors.

onc, onco, oncodoc oncologist.

Oncoseed (Nycomed Amersham): brand name for the I-125 seed implant.

oncostatin M cytokine of the interleukin; produced by actuated T-cells; inhibits tumor cell growth.

open biopsy surgical procedure in which a sample of tissue is obtained during the surgery.

OPFS objective progression-free and overall survival.

oral chelation therapy (OCT) therapy in which the patient takes chelation (remove ionic elements from the blood) pills.

oral transmucosal fentanyl citrate (OTFC) *see* **Actiq**.

orchialgia pain in a testicle.

orchiectomy (orch) surgical removal of the testicles; certain drugs or radiation can result in a nonsurgical orchiectomy.

organ well-defined structure in the body composed of a group of tissues that work in concert to carry out a specific set of functions; for example, the heart, lungs, or prostate.

orgasm sexual climax; accompanied by ejaculation in men.

OS overall survival.

osteoarthritis degeneration of the cartilage and bones of the joints.

osteoblast cell that forms bone.

osteoclast cell that breaks down bone-cell growth in bony tissue; apparently absorbs bone tissue.

osteolysis destruction of bone.

osteolytic characterized by decrease in bone density, which may show up on a bone scan.

osteonectin (National Institute of Dental and Craniofacial Research): protein primarily present in bone; attracts prostate cancer cells and promotes invasiveness; *under study.*

osteoporosis change in bone; usually decreased density and increased brittleness that occurs with age, calcium loss, and hormone depletion.

osteosclerotic characterized by increased bone density; may show on a bone scan.

OTC over-the-counter drugs; nonprescription drugs.

outpatient term which refers to treatment that does not involve an overnight stay, either in a hospital or medical office.

overall survival time from the primary treatment of a cancer to the death of the patient.

overflow incontinence condition in which the urinary bladder retains urine after voiding; as a consequence, the bladder remains full most of the time, resulting in involuntary seepage of urine from the bladder.

overstaging assignment of a higher clinical stage at initial diagnosis because of the difficulty of assessing the available information with accuracy; for example, stage T3b as opposed to stage T2b.

ovoloctovegetarians will not eat meat or any other animal products; including milk, cheese, and eggs.

oxybutynin chloride *see* **Ditropan XL**.

Oxycontin (Purdue Pharma L.P.): drug that acts as a pain reliever with no ceiling as to quantity required to control pain.

oxygen *see* **hyperoxygenation therapy**.

P

p2p physician to patient.

p27 protein tumor marker that may indicate whether prostate cancer is progressing quickly or slow growing; can possibly predict when localized prostate cancer is likely to return after treatment: researchers discovered that prostate cancer cells, with lower levels of p27, were more aggressive; *under study.*

p53 (University of Texas, Austin): tumor-suppressor gene with complex functions; as cancer progresses and spreads, the gene may have mutations and lose the power to trigger damaged cells to go into programmed cell death or apoptosis; *under study.*

pa2024 fusion protein composed of prostatic acid phosphatase and a dendritic cell targeting element being tested for hormone refractory prostate cancer; *under study.*

pp32 gene that was found to be switched on in normal cells, but generally off in cancer cells; early studies show that pp32 acts as a suppressor and keeps cells from turning malignant; *under study.*

pp32r1, pp32r2 genes that are present in approximately 90 percent of the prostate cancers studied; *under study.*

paclitaxel (Bristol Myers Squibb/UCSF No. 98558): ingredient in taxol which claims to improve delivery of the anti-cancer drug when given as an injection in combination with estramustine phosphate and carboplatin; *under study.*

palladium-103 (P-103) (Indigo Medical/Theragenics): radioactive isotope used in seed implants.

palliative relieving a problem without necessarily solving it; palliative therapy is given in order to relieve symptoms and improve quality of life, but is not intended to cure the patient.

palpable capable of being felt during a physical examination by a physician; palpable abnormalities of the prostate can be felt during a digital rectal examination.

pamidronate *see* **bisphosphonates, Aredia**.

panax ginseng Chinese herb, one of eight in the herbal formula *PC SPES*; may enhance immunity by stimulating the activity of natural-killer cells; studies with laboratory rats have indicated that this herb increases testosterone levels while decreasing prostate weight.

pancytopenia decrease in all the formed (cellular) elements of the circulating blood, decreased platelet, white blood cell, and red blood cell count.

PAP *see* **prostatic acid phosphatase**.

parathyroid hormone (PTH) (Department of Veterans Affairs, Little Rock, Arkansas): normal hormone produced by the pituitary gland; extracts are being injected in mice and bovines to study effect on bone metabolism; *under study.*

parsley herb/root *Petroselini herba/radix* herb used to flush out the urinary tract: *see* **German Commission E**; herb/root approved, seed **Not approved**.

parsley seed *Petroselini fructus* herb used for ailments of the lower urinary tract: *see* **German Commission E, Not approved**.

partial response (PR) decline of PSA value by approximately 50 percent from baseline for three successive evaluations taken two weeks apart.

Partin Tables tables that use PSA, Gleason score, and clinical stage of prostate cancer to predict the likelihood of organ confinement, as well as capsule, seminal-vesicle, and lymph-node involvement.

Partin II Tables tables that use PSA growth rate after prostatectomy to distinguish local recurrence from distant metastases.

pathogenesis cellular mechanisms that occur in disease development.

pathologist physician who specializes in the examination of tissues and body fluids to determine what diseases are present, their status, to determine appropriate treatment.

pathology branch of medicine concerned with disease, especially structural and functional effects in the body.

-pathy suffix meaning **disease**.

patient-controlled analgesia patient controlled intravenous infusion containing a prescribed amount of a pain relieving medication

pau d'arco tea from the inner bark of the tabebuia, an evergreen tree native to Central and South America; the tabebuia wood contains lapachol, which has been demonstrated to have antitumor effects in some animal studies, but there have been no studies on humans; *also called* **taheebo, lapacho, morado, ipe roxo** and **ipes**.

PC-3 cells androgen-independent human prostatic cancer cell line.

p.c.5 Tianjang herbal blend that may be useful after hormone therapy becomes refractory.

PC primary-care physician.

PC prostate cancer.

Pca prostate cancer.

PC digest (PCD) summary of a patient's clinical information that focuses on those medical issues that are important to evaluation and treatment decisions; often placed on messages after the signature line as a reminder to the reader; for example; Dx (2/95), age (54 yrs), Gleason score (3 plus 4), clinical stage (T2a).

PCF post-conservative therapy failure.

PCNA proliferating cell nuclear antigen; an index of cell proliferation.

PCOS prostate cancer outcomes study; evaluation of diagnostic and treatment practices of prostate cancer diagnosis in order to evaluate long-term urinary, bowel and sexual function complications after initial treatment.

PCPT prostate cancer prevention trial; to determine if the drug Finasteride can prevent prostate cancer.

PCR *see* **polymerase chain reaction**.

PC SPES (Botanic) (UCSF No. 98554): brand-name dietary supplement used to lower PSA in prostate cancer; prepared from extracts of seven Chinese herbs and one concentrated American herb; each herb is processed separately and then combined to yield a highly synergistic formula; *under study.*

PD *see* **poorly differentiated**.

PDQ physician's data inquiry.

PDR physicians' desk reference, a compilation of all prescription drugs.

PE pulmonary embolus, (clot).

peacock delivery system for intensity modulated radiation therapy (IMRT).

Pecta-sol brand name for a modified citrus pectin product.

pedigree diagram illustrating the transmission of genetic traits over several generations.

Peenuts brand name product that stands for Power to Empty Everytime while Never Urinating Too Soon; all-natural, with 15 ingredients including antioxidants, immune boosters; for prostatitis.

pelvic area basin shaped cavity continuing and protecting the bladder, rectum and reproductive organs.

pelvic node dissection removal of possible regional nodes near the prostate; to limit the spread of the cancer of the prostate; evaluation prior to a radical prostatectomy.

pelvis that part of the body that joins the lower limbs to the body.

penectomy surgery to remove all or part of the penis.

penetrance the possibility that a given gene will actually result in a disease.

Penicillamine antiangiogenesis drug in clinical trial; *under study.*

penile of the penis.

penile prosthetic implant device inserted in the penis that allows for an erection.

penile wart growth on the penis, known medically as condyloma, caused by a virus.

penis male organ of sexual intercourse, in mammals it is also the organ through which urine is ejected.

pentosan polysulfate sodium *see* **Elmiron**.

peptides an amino acid; a building block of proteins; found naturally in human blood and urine.

percutaneous through the skin.

perineal of the perineum.

perineal prostatectomy surgical removal of the prostate gland through an incision between the anus and scrotum.

perineum in a male, the area between the scrotum and the rectum.

peripheral zone outermost area of the prostate that can be felt during a digital rectal exam; comprises about 65 percent of the prostatic volume.

periprostatic tissue tissue surrounding the prostate gland; if this tissue is cancerous, the tumor is not confined or localized to the prostate gland.

permixon *liposterolic* (Nutraceutical Corp., Ogden, Utah) extract of saw palmetto berry; *under study.*

per os by mouth.

PET *see* **positron-emission tomography**.

Peyronie's disease plaque buildup along the walls of the erectile tissue of the penis resulting in scarring.

PFP progression free probability.

PFR peak flow rate.

pharmaceutical names drug generally has three names; *generic*: the biochemical ingredient responsible for drug efficacy; *chemical name*: specific for the molecule; *brand or trade name*: trademark given by the manufacturer.

pharmacogenetics genetically determined responses to drugs.

pharmacognostics branch of pharmacology that studies the natural or chemical history of unprepared medicines.

pharmacokinetics study of how a drug is absorbed and utilized in the body.

pharmacology study of drugs and their effects on living organisms.

pharmodynamics study of drug reactions.

phase I "first time in humans" trial to ascertain if a drug is safe and at what dose; the phase series usually starts after years of laboratory testing, followed by trials on animals phase I trials usually involve fewer than a hundred participants.

phase II a small-scale test of a drug's efficacy on human beings who are sick; usually involves a number of volunteers randomly selected as study and control groups.

phase III large clinical trial using volunteers randomly selected, grouped for study and control to test the safety and efficacy of drug in dosages that will be eventually administered; results are compared with the prevailing standard treatment and/or a placebo.

phase IV after approval of a drug, an ongoing study of its safety and efficacy; results are reported to the drug manufacturer and/or to the appropriate government regulatory agency.

phenazopydrine *see* Pyridium tablets.

phenolic acid antioxidant that affects enzyme activity and may inhibit formation of the carcinogen nitrosamine; sources are parsley, carrots, whole grains, and berries.

Phenylacetate drug; when given by infusion, may suppress tumor growth; *under study.*

phosphatase acid (phos) enzyme present in the prostate gland, which is elevated in cancer of the prostate.

phosphorous part of the blood-chemistry panel test: value may reflect metastatic tumor to the bone; a major component of the mineral phase of bone and occurs in all tissues, being involved in almost all metabolic processes.

photon beam radiation low-level laser therapy that transforms light of various frequencies into a very small and intense beam that produces very high heat and power.

PHSRN (University of Michigan): a cancer-inhibiting peptide, or chain of amino acids, part of a blood protein called fibronectin; *under study.*

phytochemicals soybean component.

phyto-estrogens plant version of the hormone estrogen; a compound which may increase the sex hormone binding levels of free testosterone and lower prostate cancer growth rates; *under study.*

phyto-estrogen estrogen derived from soy, which may play a role in both the prevention and spread of hormone-dependent prostate cancers.

phytosterol constituent of legumes (bean family) structurally similar to cholesterol; *see* **phytotherapy**.

phytotherapeutic agents plant delivered substances.

phytotherapy plant-derived preparation, called phytosterols, that is used for therapeutic and preventive purposes in benign prostatic hyperplasia.

pifithrin-alpha (PFTa) (University of Illinois at Chicago/Quark): compound that temporarily disables the p53 gene that is responsible for apoptosis (programmed cell death); name is an abbreviation for p-53 inhibitor; *under study: see* **apoptosis**.

pilot study small-scale investigative study of methods and procedures that, if promising, will be adopted for a larger scale study.

PIN prostatic intraepithelial neoplasia; a pathologically identifiable finding believed to be a precursor of prostate cancer; also known as *dysplasia*: *see* **atypia, dysplasia**.

PINS prostate intervention nutrition study; prostate cancer patients are randomized to one of three treatments: dietary intervention, a low fat diet and/or a combination of soy powder, selenium and Vitamin E; *under study.*

pituitary gland gland at the base of the brain; produces hormones stimulating release of testosterone, among other hormones.

PIVOT prostate cancer intervention versus observation trial; study of comparison between radical prostatectomy and palliative management for clinically localized prostate cancer; *under study.*

placebo form of safe, but nonactive treatment, frequently used as a basis for comparison with pharmaceuticals in research studies.

placebo effect occurrence in clinical trials in which people receiving a placebo, (nonactive treatment), actually show improvement in their condition.

plantain *Plantago asiatic* herb that may stimulate natural killer-cell activity.

plasma pale, amber-colored, fluid portion of the blood and lymph.

plasmid small piece of DNA.

plasminogen protein, involved in blood clotting, that occurs naturally in the body; *see* **angiostatin, endostatin**.

platelet disk-shaped structure (thrombocyte) found in the circulating blood that has a role in coagulation; platelets prevent bleeding and are important in blood clot formation as a result of injury.

platelet aggregation test to evaluate the clumping tendency of platelets in the blood.

platelet count part of the complete blood count: the number of platelets in the blood are counted.

Platelet factor 4 antiangiogenesis drug; *under study.*

PLCO prostate, lung, colorectal, and ovarian cancer trial, a 16-year screening study.

PLGF placental growth compound; a protein known to activate the endothelial cell: *see* **endothelial cells** and **VEGF**.

ploidy number of sets of chromosomes in a cell; a human cell has 46 chromosomes in its nucleus: *see* **diploid** and **aneuploid**.

ploidy analysis method used to tell the degree of abnormality of the DNA complement of cancer cells; abnormal ploidy is associated with aggressiveness of a cancer.

PMT pain management team.

polyerga spleen peptides that limit cancer growth and control the metabolism of the immune system.

polymer long macromolecule made of similar or identical subunits linked together.

polymerase chain reaction (PCR) in vitro method of DNA cloning; a method for amplifying specific DNA sequences.

polymorphism variation in molecules that may predict if a patient's manifestation of prostate cancer is slow or fast-growing; it may have implications in the type of treatment administrated.

polypeptides precursor in the formation of amino acids and proteins; involved in the metabolism of these compounds.

polyphenol antioxidant that may promote the production of anticancer enzymes; presently only source known is green tea.

polyploid cells which have an extra set of chromosomes; such may indicate an abnormal cell may be cancerous.

polysaccharide complex carbohydrate compound that is obtained by water extraction; may inhibit the growth of cancer cells.

Polysulfated polysaccharide from seaweed cell walls; antiangiogenesis drug; *under study.*

polyuria excessive urine excretion.

Polyvalent antibody inducing vaccine (Memorial Sloan-Kettering) antiangiogenesis drug; *under study.*

poorly differentiated pathologic term used to describe cells which are no longer microscopically recognizable as originating from a particular cell type: in prostate cancer, these could refer to tumors with a Gleason 4 and/or 5 score; poorly differentiated tumors are more aggressive that those tumors in which the cells are more readily identified as to origin.

Porges urospiral temporary intraurethral stent (tube) used to permit restoration of voiding.

positive (POS) used to describe a test result that shows the presence of the substance or material for which the test was carried out; for example, a positive bone scan would indicate bone metastases.

Positron emission tomography (PET) type of X-ray that uses two radio tracer drugs to locate and determine tumor activity.

posterior the rear; for example, the posterior lobe of the prostate is the portion of the prostate gland that faces a man's back.

post void drip loss of a few drops of urine after the main stream has been finished; medical term is *postmicturition dribbling.*

post void residual volume amount of urine remaining in the bladder after urinating; a high volume is a sign of bladder obstruction or retention.

potassium part of the blood-chemistry panel test: an important element for muscle and nerve function. Metabolism is largely controlled by the kidneys; value is watched very closely in patients taking diuretics or cardiovascular medications: if the blood sample is not processed properly, high values may occur from cell hemolysis or breakdown.

PP Partin prediction; *see* **Partin Tables**.

PR *see* **partial response**.

PrCa prostate cancer.

PRECISE large study of 52,000 subjects using various doses of selenium supplementation; goal is the determination of the optimal level for cancer prevention, including prostate cancer; *under study.*

Prednisone (Merz): steroidal drug compound used for treatment of advanced prostate cancer patients; *under study.*

PremPro estrogen/medroxyprogesterone acetate (Wyeth-Ayerst): hormonal combination protocol in patients who become refractory to standard hormone therapy.

priapism painful and unwanted erection that lasts for an extended period of time.

prilinks-D urine test that measures breakdown of bone matrix; used to evaluate for excessive bone resorption and possible bone loss.

primary cancer cancer that originates at a specific site in the body, instead of having spread from another site; prostate cancer is a primary cancer.

prinomastat *see* **AG 3340**.

prit pretargeted radioimmuno therapy

PRL *see* **prolactin**.

proanthoeyandin antioxidant found in cat's claw and hawthorn.

procedure course of action; in medicine, a treatment or surgery.

procrit erythropoeitin (Ortho Biotech/Johnson & Johnson): natural glycoprotein that stimulates red blood cell production.

proctitis inflammation of the rectum; may be a side effect of radiation therapy.

prodrug compound that is converted within the body into its active form that has medical effects.

progenitor (SmithKline Beecham): investigating study of prostate cancer genes; *under study.*

progesterone hormone made within the ovaries; also available as a commercial natural product derived from the Mexican wild yam root; normalizes blood clotting, may restore libido, and stimulate reversal of osteoporosis; also being used to treat prostate cancer: *see* **Prometrium**.

progesterone cream being tested privately for improvement in gynecomastia; breast enlargement and/or tenderness.

prognosis prediction of the course of a disease.

programmed cell death *see*: **apoptosis**.

PROGRESS prostate cancer genetic research study (NIH/ CaPCure): prostate cancer genetic study for families with 3 or more relatives related by blood, with prostate cancer, 3 or more generations affected by PC, and/or 2 relatives, related by blood, diagnosed with PC by age 60.

progression continuing growth or regrowth, e.g. of the cancer; three consecutive increases in PSA to more than 50 percent above nadir value; as used in a nontechnical urological research plan.

prolactin (PRL) trophic hormone produced by the pituitary gland that modulates prostatic androgen receptors, increases sensitivity to androgens, and regulates production and secretion of citrate.

prolactin test related to estrogenic activity; used to evaluate gynecomastia and some other types of metabolic disorders.

proliferating cell nuclear antigen (PCNA) biomarker used to quantify cell proliferation.

Prometrium progesterone (Solvay): progesterone hormone used in replacement therapy: *see* **progesterone**.

Proscar finasteride (Merck): inhibitor of the enzyme, *5 alpha reductase*: often prescribed as part of a complete androgen blockade; used to treat complications of benign prostatic hyperplasia.

prost 30 MOAB (mAB) murine monoclonal antibody; a complex immunologically active protein carefully targeted to reach specific sites in specific organs; *under study.*

prostaglandin chemical released by the body which gives a sense of well-being.

prostaglandin e1 (PGe1) natural compound that increases the cavernous artery inflow, dilates sinusoidal muscles and restricts venous outflow promoting erectile activity; *under study*: *see* **Caverject, Edex** and **Muse**.

prostaglandin e2 (PGe2) compound derived from arachidonic acid; may disable or kill immune cells important in controlling cancer; *under study.*

Prostascint image in which a monoclonal antibody with great affinity for prostatic tissue, in particular, malignant tumors, is combined with a radioactive material (Indium 111); substance is injected intravenously and allowed to "settle" for 3 days; the radio-labeled antibody preferentially attaches itself to existing lesions. When the body is scanned, these lesions are detected by the radioactive emissions; used to help determine how far a tumor has spread.

Prostasure test that analyzes five biomarkers in relation to the patient's age in an attempt to identify a pattern consistent with disease.

Prostata brand-name herbal product made from liquid squeezed from the reddish berries of the saw palmetto; manufacturer claims it helps maintain a healthy prostate and may reduce prostate enlargement.

prostate walnut-size gland surrounding the urethra and located immediately below the urinary bladder in males; it produces about one-third of the fluid that makes up the semen.

prostate cancer adenocarcinoma of the prostate gland.

prostatectomy surgical removal of part or all of the prostate gland.

Prostate Formula brand-name product used as a dietary supplement.

prostate gland *see* **prostate**.

Prostate, lung, colon, ovarian (PLCO) (NCI): clinical trial which randomizes men to screening with PSA and DRE versus no screening.

prostate massage stroking the prostate using a finger inserted through the rectum in order to obtain a sample of prostatic fluid for examination.

Prostate-specific antigen (PSA) protein secreted by the epithelial cells of the prostate gland, including cancer cells; an elevated level in the blood indicates an abnormal condition of the prostate gland, either benign or malignant; used to detect potential problems in the prostate gland and to follow the progress of prostate cancer therapy. It is recommended that the PSA blood sample be taken prior to a DRE, biopsy, or any other form of prostatic manipulation; *see* **screening**.

Prostate-specific antigen type II (free PSA, PSA II) reports the percentage of free PSA to total PSA (total PSA = free PSA + bound PSA); helpful for screening purposes when PSA values are above the normal, but less than 10.

prostate stones calculi (stones) which are usually composed of calcium within the prostate gland.

prostate zone one of the four regions of the prostate gland; i.e. central, periurethral, peripheral, and transition.

prostatic acid phosphatase (PAP) enzyme measured to evaluate the possibility that prostate cancer has metastasized; PAP is not elevated unless the tumor has spread outside the anatomic prostatic capsule.

prostatic ducts group of 20 to 30 channels inside the prostate that collect and transport prostatic fluid to the ejaculatory ducts.

prostatic infarction tissue death; usually the result of a blockage of the blood supply to a portion of the prostate gland.

prostatic stent wire coil that is inserted into the prostatic urethra to maintain flow.

prostatic urethra section of the urethra that passes through the prostate.

prostatitis infection or inflammation of the prostate gland; treatable by medication, manipulation, or both: *see* **benign prostatic hyperplasia**.

prostatodynia inflammation of the prostate gland causing pain.

prostatosis disorder of the prostate, with symptoms of prostatitis, in which no infectious microorganisms are detected by laboratory or culture.

prostatovesiculectomy surgical removal of the seminal vesicles along with the prostate gland.

Prostatron (EDAP): use of heat to shrink the prostate without damaging the surrounding tissue; protocol has been extensively used in England and France. Hyperthermia of the prostate gland is currently not an approved procedure in the USA, but is being investigated: *see* **hyperthermia, TUMT**.

Prostavan melalevca: brand name product contains saw palmetto berry, pumpkin seed and lycopene; claims to promote proper urinary function.

prosthesis synthetic device used to replace a normal body part or function.

Prost-Mate brand name product made of saw palmetto, lycopene, green tea extract, pumpkin seed powder, and an extract of the Japanese mushroom, *Grifola frondosa.*

ProstRcision radiation prostatectomy; radioactive seeds are implanted directly into the prostate using ultrasound technology: three weeks after the implantation, the patient undergoes external radiation.

prostvac prostate specific gene that targets the immune system against prostate cancer cells; *under study.*

protein substance found in all living matter and necessary for the growth and repair of animal tissue; proteins are comprised of amino acids as their basic structural units.

proteinchip (Ciphergen Biosystems): technology that finds protein "fingerprints" for multiple forms of prostate or other types of cancer; system utilizes laser capture microdissection to extract cells to be used to monitor disease progression; *under study.*

protocol written, predetermined set of methods by which a research study is to be carried out.

proton beam radiation procedure that may use as many as 12 beams of radiation to treat tumors: proton subparticles are absorbed by the tumor, instead of emerging through the lesion.

proton beam therapy form of radiation using protons to treat cancer patients; the proton beam is focused on the site of the cancer; protons are elementary particles found in the nuclei of all atoms, rather than X-ray radiation.

proto-oncogenes genes that encode for a variety of proteins involved in normal cell growth and proliferation.

pruritus itchiness caused by irritation of the skin.

PSA *see* **prostate-specific antigen**.

PSA II *see* **prostate-specific antigen type II**.

PSA age-specific suggested level based on age.

PSA density (PSAD) formula in which the PSA is divided by the size or volume of the prostate.

PSA doubling time (PSADT) time it takes the PSA to double in value; an index of the aggressiveness of a tumor.

PSA, Hybritech tandem PSA test, approved by the FDA as a diagnostic tool.

PSA Immulite (Diagnostic): third-generation assay, an ultrasensitive test with a low analytical detection limit.

PSA RT-PCR PSA reverse transcriptase-polymerase chain reaction; blood test that detects micrometastatic cells circulating in the bloodstream; may be useful as a screening tool to help avoid unnecessary invasive treatments on patients with metastasized prostate cancer.

PSARV PSA relative velocity.

PSA velocity (PSAV) rate at which PSA values increase or decrease.

PSA with urokinase serine protease, from the kidney, secreted by prostatic epithelium, (lining of vessels); may be involved in the splitting of protein cascade during prostate cancer invasion and metastasis.

PSCA prostate stem cell antigen, a prostate-specific cell-surface antigen.

psm prostate-specific membrane, a membrane that surrounds the protoplasm; entire contents of a live cell.

PSMA prostate-specific membrane antigen, a diagnostic prostate marker.

PSM RT-PCR assay that tests for a PSM glycoprotein derived from the cell membrane of the human prostatic cancer cell line LNCaP; may give high results for hormone-refractory disease.

psychic surgery illusion that surgery has been performed utilizing a red dye to simulate blood; practiced in Brazil and the Philippines.

psychological methods various techniques such as imagery, meditation, progressive muscle relaxation, and psychotherapy: in general, such techniques may reduce stress, alleviate depression, help control pain, and improve a patient's quality of life, but it is not known if they influence the course of disease.

psyllium seed husk *Ovatae testa plantaginis* major source of fiber, used both for diarrhea and constipation: *see* **German Commission E**.

PT prothrombin time blood test frequently used to evaluate coagulation by Coumadin users.

pten (Memorial Sloan Kettering): gene that normally combats cancer by killing abnormal cells that could form tumors; when one of the normal pair of PTEN genes is missing or flawed, the single mutation can trigger cancer; *under study: also called* **MMAC1**.

PTH parathyroid hormone one of the principal calcium regulating hormones in the body.

PTHrP parathyroid hormone related protein.

PT1-00703 (Proteo Tech): experimental cat's claw compound.

pts patients.

pubococcygeus muscles located near the rectum; Kegel exercises are designed to strengthen these muscles.

pumpkin seed *Cucurbitae peponis semen* herb used for relief of an irritable bladder; also relieve symptoms associated with an enlarged prostate in stage 1 and 2, but does not reduce the enlargement itself: *see* **German Commission E**.

PV prostate volume.

PVR postvoid residual ultrasound, a test to determine amount of urine left in bladder after urination.

pygeum africanum herb which is not as effective as saw palmetto; may have additional side effects in addition to those of saw palmetto.

Pyridium tablets phenazopydrine (DuPont Merck): drug that may help to relieve painful urination.

Pyrilinks-D a urine test.

Q

Qd once each day, to be taken about the same time each day.

qid. four times each day, about every six hours.

Quadramet samarium-153 (Cytogen): injectable radiotherapy treatment to minimize pain of bone metastases.

quality of life (QOL) evaluation of the state of well being relative to a patient's age, expectations, life-style, physical and mental capabilities.

quantitative nuclear grade (QNG) (UroCor): testing and analysis procedure that may be able to predict whether men who have had prostate cancer are likely to have recurrence after treatment; *under study*: *see* **GENN**.

R

rl0903 (Roberts): hydrogel implant technology use of a LHRH agonist for hormonal treatment of prostate cancer; implant delivers therapeutic agents at a controlled, constant release rate for up to one year; *under study*.

rabdosia rubescens Chinese herb, one of eight in the herbal formula *PC SPES*, with multiple antitumor and analgesic effects.

race population that differs from others in the relative frequency of some gene or genes; the incidence rate of prostate cancer is almost twice as high among blacks as among whites; Asians have the lowest incidence.

race-specific PSA reference ranges PSA ranges based on a man's racial background; this led to "race-specific reference ranges" for determining normal PSA reference levels.

rad old unit of radiation dose now superseded by the gray (1 gray = 100 rads).

rad, rays radiotherapy.

radiation any form of electromagnetic energy wave of any stream of electrically charged atoms or molecules; radiation can include heat, light, magnetism, sound, as well as X-rays.

radiation oncologist physician specializing in the treatment of cancer using different types of radiation therapy.

radiation protectors shields to protect normal tissues around the area being treated.

radiation therapy (RT) use of high-energy X-rays, or other forms of radiation, to destroy cancer cells, thus shrinking tumors; radiation may originate from a machine outside the body, (external radiation therapy), from radioactive materials surgically implanted, or ingested radioactive material, (internal radiation therapy).

radical in a surgical sense, a bold approach directed at the cause of a disease; thus, radical prostatectomy is the surgical removal of the entire prostate gland with the intent to "cure" the disease.

radical cystectomy surgical removal of all or part of the urinary bladder.

radical perineal prostatectomy (RPP) surgical procedure to remove the prostate gland from a surgical opening in the perineum, the area between the anus and scrotum.

radical prostatectomy (RP) operation to remove the entire prostate gland and seminal vesicles.

radical retropubic prostatectomy (RRP) operation in which the prostate gland and seminal vesicles are removed through the lower abdomen.

radioactive-seed implantation *see* **brachytherapy**.

radioimmunotherapy treatment using radioactive antibodies which are injected into a patient to search out the tumor cells and destroy them.

radioisotope unstable atom that decays to a stable state by emitting radiation; such radiation can be used to kill cancer cells by damaging their DNA; some are also used to visualize particular organs, as in a nuclear scan.

radiologist physician who specializes in diagnosing diseases through the use of radiation therapy, such as X-rays.

radionuclide scintigraphy *see* **bone scan**.

radiosensitivity degree to which cancer or other cells respond to radiation.

radiosensitizers drugs which are used to make tumors more sensitive to radiation.

radiotherapeutic use of radiotherapy in controlling disease.

radiotherapy *see* **radiation therapy**.

raloxifene *see* **Evista**.

R & D research and development.

randomized nonselective process of assigning patients to different forms of treatment in a research study.

rapid saliva prostate cancer test saliva collected with a sponge is applied to a test strip; the PSA level is indicated by a pink line on the strip within 15 minutes; PSA blood test level may also be used to confirm results.

ras family of genes that encode for similar cell membrane bound proteins that are involved in signal transduction: *see* **oncogene**.

RBC red blood count: *see* **red cell count**.

RBC morphology part of complete blood count: the size and shape of the red blood cells as obtained from a blood sample.

RCC *see* **red cell count**.

RCT randomized controlled trial.

RCV red cell volume; *see* **Hemocrit**.

RD registered dietician.

RDA recommended daily allowance.

receptor openings on the surface of cells that permit certain substances to enter the cell.

recommended daily allowance (RDA) quantity of a vitamin or mineral established by the Food and Nutrition Board of the National Academy of Sciences to "meet the needs of practically all healthy persons."

rectal exam *see* **digital rectal exam**.

rectum last part of the large intestine, which ends at the anus.

recurrence reappearance of disease after a period of remission.

red cell count part of a complete blood count: number of red cells found in the circulating blood; the red blood cells carry oxygen in the blood; low results are commonly associated with certain types of anemia; *also known* as erythrocyte count.

reflexology alternate therapy involving massage of the feet and hands; proponents believe that pressure applied to different points of the back will positively affect other body sites.

refractory resistant to therapy; for example, hormone-refractory prostate cancer is resistant to some forms of hormonal treatment.

regional involvement spread of cancer from its original site to anatomic surrounding areas, such as regional lymph nodes; confined to one location of the body.

registry, cancer central or regional facility which compiles reports of cancer patients as to location, type, treatment regimens after their initial diagnosis and periodic follow-up on patient's status.

regression reduction in the number and/or size of tumors.

rehabilitation program directed to help patients adjust to, and recover from, the effects of cancer; may involve physical therapy, counseling, and emotional support.

relapse reappearance of cancer after a disease-free period.

remission real or apparent disappearance of some or all of the signs and symptoms of cancer; the period (temporary or permanent) during which disease remains under control, that is, without clinical progression; complete remission does not necessarily indicate cure.

renal cell cancer tumor arising from the cells of the kidney, in contrast to those arising from the transitional cells of the urinary collecting system.

reolysin (Synsorb Biotech): reovirus that may be able to selectively kill human cancer cells in vitro, (test tube), from prostate, breast, pancreatic and brain tumors; *understudy*: *see* **reovirus**.

reovirus respiratory enteric orphan (University of Calgary): naturally occurring virus that may be a killer of cancer cells; *under study*.

resection surgical removal of portion or all of a part of the body.

resectoscope surgical instrument, utilized by a urologist, to visualize and remove tissue (usually from the prostate, urinary bladder neck, etc.); technique used to treat urinary obstruction by an enlarged prostate: *see* **transurethral resection of the prostate**.

residual urine that quantity of urine remaining in the urinary bladder after voiding is completed.

resistance in a medical sense, patient's ability to fight off a disease as a result of the effectiveness of the patient's immune system; may include other compounds such as nutrition, and heredity.

resorption process of utilizing ingested substances or those removed during metabolism; for example, calcium is continuously deposited in bone and reabsorbed into the circulating blood system, then redeposited, etc.

response effectiveness of therapy; the desired effect is one of positive response, that is one that cures or diminishes the disease status.

resting secretion normal rate of prostatic fluid secretion without any erotic stimulation.

retinoic acids compound that may be helpful as a differentiative agent in prostate cancer; derivative of, or closely related to vitamin A; includes all trans-retinoic acid (ATRA): *see* **Atragen.**

retro ejaculation flow of semen into the urinary bladder on ejaculation, rather than from the penis; *also known as* **dry ejaculation**.

retropubic prostatectomy surgical removal of the prostate through an incision in the lower abdomen: *see* **suprapubic**.

retrovirus virus with RNA as its genetic material; can be translated into DNA; retroviruses may cause cancers and other diseases.

reverse transcriptase enzyme that changes RNA to DNA in white blood cells.

reverse transcriptase polymerase chain reaction a technique that allows a physician to search for tiny quantities of a protein, such as PSA, in the blood, other body fluids or tissues. Since current reproducibility is poor, test results are reported as "positive" or "negative" rather than in quantitative ranges: *see* **PSA RT-PCR**.

Revia naltrexone hydochloride (DuPont): *Not to be confused with Nalexone.* drug which may restore normal immune system function in prostate cancer patients by inhibiting the growth of tumor cells: tested privately for prostate cancer in low dosage of 3 mg; higher dosage approved by FDA in 1989 to treat opiate addictions; *under study*: *see* **endorphin**.

Revici, Emanuel, M.D. physician who developed a system of chemotherapy using lipid-based substances, selenium compounds, sterols, alcohol, female hormones, amines, nicotinic acid derivatives, metals, and halogens; dosages were unique for each patient and administered orally or by injection.

RH releasing hormone.

Rhenium 186 (RE186) radioisotope helpful in reducing symptoms of bone pain.

rhizotomy severing of a sensory nerve where it enters the spinal cord.

RIA radio immunoassay.

ribonucleic acid (RNA) molecule within a cell nucleus that maintains the genetic codes that insure healthy cell division.

ribosome cell machinery for making proteins.

Rife, Royal Raymond scientist, who in 1920, developed electromagnetic energy therapy; he claimed frequency vibrations would cause the cancer virus to self-destruct; a current version of this therapy uses a modified CB radio to transmit radio signal pulses from an audio-frequency generator; the signal is then amplified to about 100 w of power; this AM radio signal is fed into a modified radio antenna to light a "plasma" tube, which is claimed to radiate energy into the area where the patient sits. Such pulse waves are supposed to find the cells causing the problem, and vibrate them until they are destroyed.

risedronate *see* **Actonel**.

risk factor condition that increases an individual's chance of developing a disease; such as cancer.

risk ratio ratio of the incidence of disease or death among those exposed to a risk factor relative to those who are unexposed.

risk reduction techniques used to reduce an individual's chance of developing a certain disease, such as reducing dietary fat to help prevent certain types of cancer.

RL 0903 (Sugen) *under study*.

RLQ right lower quadrant; term used to describe locations of the abdomen by 4 divisions, for example; right or left upper, or lower quadrants.

RNA *see* **ribonucleic acid**.

Rocaltrol calcitriol (Roche): activated vitamin D preparation that promotes absorption of calcium by bone; used for treatment of osteoporosis; usual dosage is 0.25 mcg per day, but higher doses of 0.75 to 1.5 mcg per day shown to be effective against prostate cancer.

rofecoxib *see* **Vioxx**.

RP *see* **radical prostatectomy**.

RPP *see* **radical perineal prostatectomy**.

RRP *see* **radical retropubic prostatectomy**.

RT *see* **radiation therapy.**

RT-PCR *see* **reverse transcriptase polymerase chain reaction**.

Rx prescription.

S

SAGE serial analysis of gene expression (Genzyme Moleculor Oncology): identification of genes as diagnostic markers and therapeutic targets for potential cancer product development.

saha (Memorial Sloan Kettering): compound which prompts prostate cancer cells to resume normal cell functions; study involves in vitro and in vivo protocols; binds with its protein target thus interfering with the activity of a key enzyme, a desired effect; *under study.*

Sailor's disease irritated prostate condition resulting from prolonged periods of sexual abstinence; *also called* **priest's disease**.

saluretic substance that increases the elimination of salts in the urine.

salvage procedure intended to "rescue" a patient following the failure of a prior treatment; for example, a salvage prostatectomy would be the surgical removal of the prostate after radiation therapy or cryosurgery has failed: cure may not be a realistic expectation of these modalities.

salvage work-up examination and tests done after cancer has recurred as an aid in choosing additional treatments.

samarium-153 *see* **Quadramet**.

sandalwood, red *Santali lignum rubrum* herb used to treat ailments of the gastrointestinal tract: *see* **German Commission E, Not approved**.

sandalwood, white *Santali lignum albi* for adjuvant therapy of infections of the lower urinary tract: *see* **German Commission E**.

Sandostatin (Novartis): growth compound inhibitor for advanced disease; *under study.*

sandwich therapy treatment protocol which allows a patient time off between treatment sequences.

saponin Chinese herb that may stimulate the immune system and inhibit the expression of the Epstein-Barr virus, which is associated with certain cancers.

sar (Abbott Labs/Idun): protocol which uses nuclear magnetic resonance spectroscopy to identify small molecule drugs that kill cancer cells by targeting the apopotic (programmed cell death) pathway; *under study.*

sarcoma form of cancer that develops in connective tissue such as bone, fat, or muscle.

saturated fats refers to the hydrogen molecules in the fatty acid chain, while primarily saturated in animals; some vegetable oils are also saturated (coconut oil, etc.). A practical way to tell is an oil that becomes solid at refrigerated temperatures; this is in contrast to "unsaturated" and "polyunsaturated" fats.

saw palmetto *Serenoa repens* Chinese herb, one of eight in the herbal formula *PC SPES;* laboratory tests indicate it decreases the bioavailability of testosterone.

saw palmetto berry *Sabal fructus* herbal extract that eases the symptoms of enlarged prostate in benign prostatic hyperplasia disease; based on 18 trials involving more than 29,000 men; *under study: see* **German Commission E; University of Texas**.

scan to systematically examine with a sensing device; such as a beam of radiation.

SCID severe combined immunodeficiency.

scintillation in nuclear; the flash of light produced when an X or gamma ray is absorbed by a radiation detector.

screening examination to separate patients with tumors from those without tumors; multiple criteria may be used: screening may be done for conditions other than cancer, such as diabetes and high blood pressure.

script prescription.

scrotum pouch or sac of skin and soft tissues containing the testicles.

scutellaria baicalensis Chinese herb, one of eight in the herbal formula *PC SPES*; has been shown in laboratory tests to inhibit the growth of tumors (sarcoma-180 cells, sarcoma-37, and cervical cancer) cells.

sea cucumber extract of sea cucumber being studied to evaluate effectiveness in blocking an enzyme that speeds up cancer progression in animal models: *see* **University of Texas**.

Seacure brand-name product of hydrolyzed fish protein, with very short chain peptides, thought to break down peptides into amino acids; used to treat digestive-tract damage from radiation therapy.

secondary site second site of metastatic cancer.

seed implantation (SI) *see* **brachytherapy**.

seed pods slang term for a person interested in brachytherapy.

seeds (University of Rochester/Rtek Medical Systems): tentative name given to a computer program to choose most effective arrangement for seed distribution; *under study*.

SEER surveillance, epidemiology and end results (NCI): protocol to track cancer incidence and mortality.

selenium relatively rare nonmetallic element found in small quantities in food; may have some effect in the prevention of prostate cancer; study showed that the group taking selenium supplements had significantly fewer cases of cancer than did the group taking a placebo: *see* **German Commission E; University of Texas**.

self-medication taking charge of your own pill-taking; not confined to pills.

semen whitish, opaque fluid emitted through the penis by a male at ejaculation.

seminal relating to semen.

seminal-vesicle involvement extension of prostate cancer into the seminal vesicles; indicates a more advanced stage of cancer.

seminal vesicles reservoir for sperm and seminal fluid; at sexual climax, the prostate contracts, causing the ejaculation of sperm with seminal fluid.

senna *Cassia garrettiana* herbal preparation used as an intestinal cleaner.

sensitivity in epidemiology, a diagnostic term used to relate the proportion of people with a disease who are accurately diagnosed by a test or procedure: *see* **specificity/sensitivity**.

Sepa alprostadil/sepa (Macro Chem): topical gel compound that delivers drugs through the human skin (direct tissue absorption) and into the bloodstream; *under study.*

sequential hormone therapy patient's response to one treatment is evaluated to determine whether other treatments are needed.

SERM selective estrogen receptor modulators synthetic compounds that have estrogenlike effects.

serum liquid that separates from whole blood upon clotting.

serum transaminase liver function test.

sex chromosome one of the two chromosomes that provide an organisms genetic sex, *see* **chromosomes**.

sextant having six parts; thus, a sextant biopsy is a biopsy that takes six representative samples.

sexual behavior no clear relationship has been established between sexual activity and prostate cancer.

sexual dysfunction not having the ability to have an erection adequate for vaginal penetration.

SF scatter factor protein known to activate the endothelial cell: *see* **endothelial cells, VEGF**.

SGOT serum glutamic oxaloacetic transaminase part of the blood-chemistry panel test ; an enzyme involved in the metabolism of the heart, muscle, and liver; alcohol consumption, liver disease, and other compounds have been shown to raise this value; low values are probably not clinically significant.

SGPT serum glutamic pyruvic transaminase part of the blood-chemistry panel test: an enzyme involved in the cellular metabolism of the heart, muscle, and liver.

shark cartilage angiogenesis (development of new blood vessels) inhibitor, which may reduce the growth of new blood vessels to new tissue masses; thus causing the tumor to starve and die. The FDA states that any claims to treat cancer has not been proved.

SHBG sexual hormone binding globulin a protein fraction in the blood.

shiitake extract extract of shiitake mushroom; shown to have very strong anticancer activities; researchers are attempting to discover the composition of these active molecules within extracts.

SI seed implantation: *see* **brachytherapy**.

side effect reaction to a medication or treatment; most commonly used to mean an undesirable effect.

sign physical change that can be observed as a consequence of an illness or disease.

signal transduction processes by which an extracellular signal; i.e., a hormone, interacts with a receptor on the cell surface, causing a change within the cell that results in a change in its function.

sildenafil *see* **Viagra**.

silent BPH growth of a benign tumor in benign prostatic hyperplasia that is not detected by the digital rectal examination.

Simonton, Carl, M.D. physician who claims that cancers can be affected by relaxation, along with a positive mental attitude; the course of a malignancy can be altered by strengthening the immune system: theory is that the brain stimulates the endocrine glands to inspire the immune system to attack cancer cells.

Sitz bath bath in which an individual sits in a few inches of hot water; used to treat various prostate and anorectal conditions.

skullcap *see* **baicalein**.

SM *see* **surgical margin**.

smart bomb drugs designed to seek out and destroy cancer cells while leaving normal cells unharmed.

sneezewort *Achillea ptarmic* in folk medicine; a drug which was used as a remedy for urinary-tract complaints.

SNP Consortium Ltd. consortium comprised of 10 drug firms researching genetic attributes that predispose people to diseases.

Social Security Death Index study to determine survival rate of cancer patients treated with Hoxsey and Livingston therapies: *see* **University of Texas, Hoxley** and **Livingston-Wheeler**.

Society for Cancer Research *see* **iscador**.

sodium part of the blood-chemistry panel test: an ion that is important in the conduction of nerve impulses, contraction of muscles, and functioning of cells.

sodium fluoride source of inorganic fluoride, which increases bone mass; according to the Mayo Clinic, oral use may increase bone mass.

Soluble FLT-1 VEGF receptor antiangiogenesis drug; *under study.*

solu-cotref hydrocortisone sodium succinate (CLB9663): study of prostate cancer cells obtained from a bone marrow biopsy for the evaluation of changes in their androgen receptors.

sonogram image produced using sound waves (ultrasound); *under study.*

sonography technique in which pictures are taken via sonogram; (ultrasound).

south African star grass *Hypoxis rooper* extract mainly contains beta-sitosterol (harzol); possibly a major active component in plant extracts; *under study.*

soy a stable food, possible cancer-prevention agent; varies from whole soy to purified extracts of phytochemicals: while whole soy contains all the anticarcinogens, extracts may deliver larger amounts of the biological active phytochemicals.

soybean extract extract of soybean has been shown to have very strong anticancer activities; researchers are attempting to discover the composition of the active molecules within the extract.

soy trials (Memorial Sloan-Kettering): clinical trials to determine if a special diet that includes soy can decrease the rate of prostate cancer.

SPARC antiangiogenesis drug; *under study.*

specificity epidemiologic term which describes the probability that a diagnostic test can correctly identify the absence of a particular disease; calculated from the number of true negative results divided by the sum of the true negative results and the false positive results; a method that detects 95 percent of true prostate cancer cases that are highly sensitive.

specificity/sensitivity term used to describe a percentage ratio between disease versus nondisease states.

specimen sample of body tissue or fluid.

sperm reproductive tadpole-shaped cell, produced in the testicles, and transported by semen.

sperm cell (University of Pennsylvania Veterinary Medicine): transplanted cell from young males who undergo cancer treatments that damage their reproductive potential; eventually develop into sperm; *under study.*

spes hope in Latin.

s-phase percentage of tumor cells actively dividing at a given point in time.

sphincter in the urinary bladder concentrically arranged muscle, that, when open, permits the urine to flow into the urethra; when the sphincter is closed, the urine is held within the bladder: sphincter muscle valves are also found in other locations.

Sphincter 800 urinary prosthesis (American Medical Systems): surgical implant to control urination.

spinal injection of a local anesthetic into the spinal cord fluid; generally limited to a desired level of anesthesia.

spiny restharrow root *Ononidis radix* herb used in irrigation therapy for inflammatory diseases of the lower urinary tract: *see* **German Commission E**.

squalamine an aminosterol, similar to the cholesterol molecule, that immobilizes calmodulin in endothelial cells causing them to stop responding to growth compounds secreted by cancer cells; *under study: see* **calmodulin, endothelial**.

squalamine lactate antiangiogenesis drug in clinical trial; *under study.*

Squeezer, The (Cochrane): brand name for an external incontinence-control clamp; *under study.*

stabilization (STAB) situation of patients who do not meet the criteria for complete, partial response or progression for at least 90 days; as used in a nontechnical urological research plan.

stage indication of the size of a tumor (or tumors), and the extent of the spread of the cancer

staging, tumor or cancer evaluation of the extent of a disease based on the stage at diagnosis; used to help determine appropriate therapy: there are two staging methods: (1) the Whitmore-Jewett staging classification (1956) and (2) the more detailed TNM (tumor, nodes, metastases) classification (1992) of the American Joint Committee on Cancer and the International Union Against Cancer

Stage A =T1 TNM (Whitmore-Jewett)

Stage B =T2

Stage C =T3

Stage D =T4

Whitmore-Jewett Stages

Stage A: clinically undetectable tumor confined to the gland; an incidental finding during prostate surgery.

A1: well-differentiated with focal involvement.

A2: moderately or poorly differentiated or involves multiple tumors in the gland.

Stage B: tumor confined to the prostate gland.

B0: nonpalpable, PSA, or digital rectal examination detected.

B1: single nodule in one lobe of the prostate.

B2: extensive involvement of one lobe or involvement of both lobes.

Stage C: tumor clinically localized to the periprostatic area but extending through the prostatic capsule; seminal vesicles may be involved.

C1: clinical extracapsular extension

C2: extracapsular tumor producing ureteral obstruction.

Stage D: metastatic disease.

D0: localized disease in the prostate, but persistently elevated phosphatase acid.

Dl: regional lymph nodes only.

D2: distant lymph nodes, metastases to bone or visceral organs.

D3: D2 prostate cancer patients who relapse after adequate hormone therapy.

TNM stages

Primary Tumor (T)

TX: primary tumor cannot be assessed.

T0: no evidence of primary tumor.

T1: clinically inapparent tumor not felt by touch or visible by imaging.

Tla: tumor present in 5 percent or less, of tissue resected.

Tlb: tumor present in more than 5 percent of tissue resected.

T1c: tumor identified by needle biopsy, (e.g., because of elevated PSA).

T2: tumor confined within the prostate.

T2a: tumor involves half a lobe or less.

T2b: tumor involves more than half a lobe, but not both lobes.

T2c: tumor involves both lobes; extends through the prostatic capsule.

T3: extension out of the prostate into the immediately surrounding tissue.

T3a: unilateral extracapsular extension.

T3b: bilateral extracapsular extension.

T3c: tumor invades the seminal vesicle(s).

T4: tumor is fixed or invades adjacent structures other than the seminal vesicles.

T4a: tumor invades bladder neck, external sphincter, or rectum.

T4b: tumor invades muscles and/or is fixed to the pelvic wall.

Regional Lymph Nodes (N)

NX: regional lymph nodes cannot be assessed.

N0: no regional lymph nodes metastasis.

N1: metastasis in a single lymph node, 2 cm or less in greatest dimension.

N2: metastasis in a single lymph node, more than 2 cm but not more than 5 cm greatest dimension, or multiple lymph-node metastases, none more than 5cm. in greatest dimension.

N3: metastasis in a lymph node more than 5 cm in greatest dimension.

Distant Metastases (M)

MX: presence of distant metastasis cannot be assessed.

M0: no distant metastasis.

M1: distant metastasis.

Mla: nonregional lymph node(s).

Mlb: bone(s).

M1c:other site(s).

Stamey sling passive implant (no mechanical mechanisms) to aid urination.

Star study of tamoxifen and raloxifene; initiated in May 1999.

steal syndrome impotence condition in which an erection is obtained, but quickly lost after insertion of the penis.

Steap Six-transmembrane epithelial antigen of the prostate (UroGenesys): target cell-surface antigen gene expressed at high levels on prostate cancers, but rarely found in non-prostate tissues; *under study*.

Steiner, Rudolph *see* **iscador**.

stent tube used by a surgeon to drain fluids; may also be used to expand a narrowed area in the urethra and other organs.

stereotactic body radiosurgery radiation treatment using a computer planning system; *also known* as **radiation stereotactic radiosurgery**.

steroid family of synthetic manufactured drugs, or body-produced natural steroids, that share a common molecular structure (6-ringed carbon atoms).

stilphosterol venous infusion used in high dose for hormone-refractory prostate cancer.

stinging nettle root *Urticae radix* herb used to treat difficulty in urination in cases of benign prostatic hyperplasia stages, 1 and 2. Marketed in Europe as Bazoton-r: *see* **German Commission E**.

stress (SUNY-Stony Brook): after correcting for age, indications are that stress levels and social support possibly indicate PSA levels; *under study*.

stress incontinence involuntary discharge of urine when there is increased pressure upon the urinary bladder, as in coughing or straining to lift heavy objects.

stricture scarring as a result of a procedure or injury) that constricts ease of flow; for example, a urethral stricture would restrict the flow of urine through the urethra; esophageal stricture would obstruct food intake to the stomach.

stroma tissue which forms the framework of an organ; cells comprising the stroma are quantitatively a much greater mass than epithelial cells which only line their surfaces.

strontium-89 *see* **Metastron**.

Su 101 leflunomide (NCI-G99/1550 Sugen): tests combine SU 1011with Novantrone in patients with stage 4 hormone refractory prostate cancer; *under study: see* **Novantrone**.

Su 5416 (Sugen): drug to control vascular endothelial growth compound, a key chemical for triggering blood-vessel growth which is common in most solid tumors; *under study.*

Su 6668 (Sugen/Pharma & Upjohn) blocks blood vessel receptors for VEGF and two other signaling proteins; *under study*: *see* **VEGF**.

substrate substance that is acted upon by an enzyme.

suicide gene gene inserted in to a cancer cell; may make it supersensitive to some drugs.

support group group of people on whom an individual can rely to provide emotional caring, concern, and reinforcement of a sense of personal value; may include provision of practical or material aid, information, guidance, feedback, and validation of the individual's stressful experiences and coping choices.

supportive care measures to relieve symptoms and improve quality of life, but not expected to destroy the cancer, e.g., pain medication.

suppressor T-cells cells triggered after other immune-systems have successfully fought off an infection.

suprapubic above the pubic area.

Suprefact buserelin (Hoescht Marion Roussel): synthetic hormone that inhibits the production of a hormone from the pituitary gland leading to a reduction in the testosterone; *under study.*

sural nerve sensory nerve located on the back of the ankle; implants of this nerve to the cavernous nerves removed during a radical prostatectomy; may prevent erectile dysfunction.

Suramin hexasodium salt (A. G. Scientific): antitumor agent for treatment of metastic hormonal-refractory prostate cancer; antiangiogenesis drug in clinical trial; *under study.*

surgical castration *see* **orchiectomy**.

surgical margin (SM) outer margin of resected tissues: in the removal of the prostate gland, the outside of the gland is inked by the surgeon; when the pathologist examines the specimen, determination is made whether any tumor cells are in contact with the inked surface; if such cells are present, it is assumed there are tumor cells left in the body.

Surlyn androderm (E I duPont): patch delivery system for testosterone.

suture surgical stitching material used in the closure of an incision or wound.

SV *see* **seminal vesicle**.

Swedish oncology group European tumor study that randomizes men with a radical prostatectomy versus watchful waiting.

sympathetic nerves one of the two divisions of the vertebrate autonomic nervous system; other is the parasympathetic nervous system.

symptom a feeling, sensation, or experience associated with, or resulting from a physical or mental disorder, that is noticeable by the patient.

symptoms of prostate cancer or BPH compiled by the National Institute of Health: symptoms include: frequent urination, inability to urinate, trouble starting to urinate or holding back urination, pain during ejaculation, weak or interrupted urine flow, pain or burning sensation during urination, blood in the semen or in the urine, or frequent pain or stiffness in the lower back, hips or upper thighs.

Synchtotron particle accelerator that delivers radiation to treat cancer; more accurate than its forerunner, the cyclotron.

SynerGene window-based software application to compare and analyze multiple genetic maps.

systemic widespread effects throughout the whole body.

systemic radiation therapy injection of radioisotopes directly into a patient's body, intended to treat a tumor.

T

T *see* **testosterone**; and **tetraploid**.

T0-T4 *see* **staging, tumor or cancer**.

TAB total androgen blockade.

Tagamet cimetidine; drug that may have immune-enhancing properties when taken as two 200-mg tablets three times a day; formerly a prescription drug, it is now sold over-the-counter.

tamarind *Tamarindus indica* preparation of the seed pods of this fruit tree may enhance trapping of white blood cells at inflammatory sites.

Tamoxifen tamoxifen acetate (Astra/Zeneca): first drug ever proven to prevent any form of cancer; may be useful with the hormonal treatment of prostate cancer to counter the effects of estrogen and reduce breast swelling: *see* **Star**.

Tamoxifen in combination with vinblastine (NCI): combination drug therapy used to treat hormone refractory prostate cancer; *under study.*

tamsulosin *see* Flomax.

tangent planned radiotherapy target used to minimize the irradiation of a sector of surrounding tissues from the target zone.

tapet (Vion): genetically engineered *salmonella* bacteria compound utilized to inhibit primary and metastatic tumors; *under study.*

targeted therapy process where T-cells kill cancer cells that carry the tumor antigen: *see* **GM-CSF.**

Targis d4 system (Urologix): system that utilizes a catheter based microwave delivery method that uniquely targets heat to destroy enlarged prostate tissue; non-surgical approach relieving benign prostatic hyperplasia symptoms.

taxanes class of chemotherapy drugs, including taxol and Taxotere.

taxol taxus brevifolia (Bristol Myers Squibb): possible cancer fighting substance from the inner bark of the Pacific yew tree; combined with retinoic acid and interferon; also produced by a semi-synthetic process from *Taxus baccata; under study: see* **beta-lapachone.**

Taxol paclitaxel chemotherapy drug, that when combined with herceptin, caused tumor regression in mice; *under study: see* **herceptin**.

Taxotere docetaxel (Rhone-Poulenc Rorer): semi-synthetic compound, belonging to the yew tree family called mitotic inhibitors; approved for refractory breast cancer.

TCAP targeted cryoablation of the prostate; a temperature monitored cryosurgical system.

T-cell white blood cell that mediates the cellular response of the human immune system in complex ways; *see* **GM-CSF**.

T-cell receptor antibody-like protein located on the surface of T-cells; binding to antigen, results in an immune response.

TCT thrombin clotting time.

TDT tumor doubling time.

technetium 99m radioactive isotope used for bone scans.

Tecogalan antiangiogenesis drug; *under study.*

T/E/D Taxotere/emcyt/decadron, combination chemotherapy program.

TeGreen Tablets brand name for a caffeine-free extract equivalent to the effects of drinking four cups of green tea.

telangiectasis dilatation (stretched beyond normal dimensions) of the capillary vessels; may be associated with recurrent episodes of bleeding.

telomerase enzyme that prevents depletion of telomeres and allows continuous cell division.

telomeres repetitive DNA strand located at the end of a chromosone; serves to protect it from damage; each time a cell divides, it loses a portion of its telomeres; eventually, a signal is sent to the cell to stop dividing: *see* **Hayflick Limit**.

terazosin *see* **Hytrin**

Terosteride drug, similar to Proscar, which may shrink the prostate, and help relieve symptoms of benign prostatic hyperplasia.

testicle *see* **testis**.

testicle transplant (New York Methodist Hospital): investigative procedure which consists of removing testicles prior to chemotherapy and radiotherapy; the glands are cryopreserved, and replaced after the desired course of therapy; *under study.*

testis testicles; one of a pair male reproductive glands located inside the scrotum; primary source of the male sex hormone testosterone: plural: testes.

Testoderm TTS C111 testeoderm (Alza): applied to the scrotal skin as a treatment for testosterone deficiency.

testosterone (T) male hormone or androgen that comprises most of the androgens in a man's body; chiefly produced by the testicles; may be produced in tissues from precursors such as androstenedione; essential to male sexual function and fertility.

tetraploid (tetra) having two sets of paired chromosomes, which is twice as many as normal. *See* **aneuploid, diploid**.

tetrathiomolybdate (TM) (University of Michigan): compound to lower copper supply in patients to deprive cancer tumors of the copper supply needed to form new blood vessels; *under study.*

tf, tn (Memorial Sloan-Kettering): carbohydrate antigen vaccines; *under study.*

TGF-B1 (Sigma-Aldrich): vaccine, being tested in rats, designed to alert the immune system by preventing tumor cells from making the beta compound that cloaks cancer cells; *under study.*

Thalidomide (NCI) polyploid chemotherapeutic drug given in oral dosage to hormonal refractory prostate cancer patients; antiangiogenesis drug; *under study.*

therapy treatment of a disease or disability.

Thera Seed (Indigo/J & J): brand name for the Palladium-103 seed implant.

Theratope *Stn-KLH* (Biomira): *under study.*

Thermotherapy (Celsion): use of focused heat in conjunction with radiation seed implant therapy; *under study.*

thrombocyte small body found in the circulating blood; important in bleeding and clotting; a platelet: *see* **platelet**.

thrombocytopenia decrease in the number of platelets in the blood; decreased platelets increases the potential for bleeding, and decreases the ability to form an adequate blood clot.

thrombospondin *see* **angiostatin**.

Thrombosporin antiangiogenesis drug; *under study.*

tid three times a day; about every eight hours.

time to disease progression period in which a disease is dormant until symptoms appear.

TIMP-1,2,3 tissue inhibitor of metalloproteinase; *see* **angiostatin**.

tin-117m dtpa diethylenetriaminepentaacetic acid (US Department of Energy, Brookhaven National Lab.): compound used as an antiangiogenesis agent to ease pain in advanced-stage bone cancer; *under study*: *see* **angiogenesis**.

tissue a coherent and functional group of cells: there are two basic types of tissue in the body, epithelial and connective.

T-lymphocyte long-lived, white blood cell responsible for cell-mediated immunity.

TNF-alpha tumor necrosis compound alpha, protein known to activate the endothelial cell; *see* **endothelial, VEGF**.

TNM system for staging cancer: T = tumor location, N = whether lymph nodes have cancer, and M = whether cancer has metastasized to other sites; *see* **staging, tumor or cancer**.

tnp-470 (Anderson Clinic, Texas/TAP): anti-angiogenesis compound to fight tumors by starving them to death, cutting off their blood supply; also known as anti-VEGF antibody; *under study*.

tolerability ability to endure the desired results as well as the side effects of a drug or treatment.

Topiglan (Northwestern University Medical School/MacroChem): topical preparation applied to the penis to relieve blood vessel constriction; *under study*.

total androgen blockade (TAB) *see* **combined androgen blockade**.

total bilirubin *see* **bilirubin panel, serum**.

total incontinence inability to control urination (failure of the bladder sphincter).

total protein part of the blood-chemistry panel test: the amount of protein circulating in the blood; this value indicates the patient's general nutritional status.

tolterodine *see* **Detrol**.

toxic symptoms of severe infection due to the nature of a poison.

toxicity side effects from an administered treatment; may range from mild to severe, are usually controllable, and in some cases, are preventable.

toxin a poison, usually from bacterial sources; may have negative effects on the body.

traditional Chinese medicine (TCM) treatment that strives to promote an overall balance within the person; herbal remedies are used to nourish the body systems and are available as capsules, pills, powders, teas, extracts, or the plant itself, and may be taken for a short or long periods: other TCMs are heat therapy, diet, exercise, massage, and meditation: *see* **University of Texas**.

Trail Tnf-related apoptosis-inducing ligand protocol being investigated to study tumor growth by directly and selectively inducing apoptosis; binds to at least four different receptors and signals these cells to destroy themselves; *under study.*

trailing arbutus *Epigae repens* herb used to treat urinary tract conditions.

Tramadol hydrochloride *see* **Ultram**.

TRAMP transgenic adenocarcinoma of mouse prostate; mouse model for cancer.

transcription converting the DNA code into a complementary messenger RNA segment

transcuntaneous nerve stimulation treatment for prostate cancer pain in which electrical impulses are applied to the affected area through the skin.

transforming growth factor beta *see* **angiostatin**.

transient incontinence temporarily induced inability to control urination, may occur in urinary infection, constipation, or reaction to medication.

transition innermost portion of the prostate that surrounds the urethra; comprises 5 to 10 percent of the prostate.

translation converting a messenger RNA sequence into a protein product.

transmucosal fentanyl citrate *see* **Actiq**.

transperineal through the perineum.

transrectal through the rectum.

transrectal ultrasound (TRUS) procedure using high frequency sound waves to image the prostate; TRUS is produced by a device inserted into the rectum; often used to guide the taking of biopsy specimens.

transurethral hyperthermia (TH) procedure which uses heat generated by a microwave transmitter to alleviate urinary obstruction in benign prostate enlargement.

transurethral laser incision of the prostate (TULIP) surgical procedure in which a laser is inserted through the urethra.

transurethral resection of the prostate (TURP) surgical procedure to remove tissue obstructing the prostatic urethra; involves the insertion of an instrument called a resectoscope into the penile urethra, intended to relieve obstruction of urine flow due to enlargement of the prostate; usually reserved for benign prostatic hyperplasis.

trastuzumab *see* **Herceptin**.

traumascan scan that uses sonogram equipment to diagnose injury to the body.

traumatic relating to, or resulting from a wound or injury, whether physical or psychological.

treatment administration of remedies to a patient for a disease.

treatment failure inability of a therapy to arrest the spread or growth of a disease or treatment.

tributyrate sodium phenylbutyrate; a potential drug remedy for cancer developed in the mid-1980s by Triple Crown America, Inc.

triglycerides part of the blood-chemistry panel test: blood fats that are absorbent and transient form of lipids in the body; values can be dramatically affected by a recent meal or physical activity: a 14 hour fast along with minimal exercise are required for accurate results.

T surge *see* **flare reaction**.

TTDP *see* time-to-disease progression.

TTND time-to-non-detectable.

TUIP transurethral incision of the prostate, surgical treatment of obstruction of the prostatic urethra by relieving bladder neck obstruction; eases urination by reducing pressure on the urethra.

TULIP *see* **transurethral laser incision of the prostate**.

tumeric *Curcuma longa* plant native to India and Indonesia; fresh tumeric seems to alleviate breast tenderness and enlargement; users claim that 20 grams mixed into a morning drink is effective; powder does not appear to be as effective.

tumor excessive growth of cells caused by uncontrolled and disorderly cell proliferation; an abnormal tissue growth that can be either benign or malignant.

tumor necrosis treatment (TNT) investigative therapy based on the utilization of a monoclonal antibody to treat bone marrow metastases.

tumor suppressor gene protective gene that usually limits the growth of tumors; *see* **p53**.

TUMT transurethral microwave thermotherapy; use of microwaves to heat and destroy excess prostate tissue.

TUNA (VidaMed): transurethral needle ablation, minimally invasive procedure for treating benign prostatic hyperplasia that requires only a local anesthetic; may have the fewest postprocedural complications of any thermal or surgical treatment of BPH.

TURP *see* **transurethral resection of the prostate**.

tyrosine amino acid present in most proteins.

Tx treatment.

U

UCI urinary clearance.

UD-PSA undetectable PSA.

ukrain alkaloid from the celeandine plant, developed in the Ukraine; currently being tested to see whether it interferes with the multiplication of cancer cells.

UL upper lobe, upper tolerable intake level.

u/l micrograms per liter (1/1,000 concentration per liter.

Ultram tramadol hydrochloride (Ortho-McNeil): drug which is approved for acute pain relief.

ultrasound far beyond the hearing range.

ultrasound-guided biopsy surgical procedure in which a biopsy is obtained by ultrasound guidance.

ultrasound therapy noninvasive therapy using sound waves of a particular frequency whose echoes are reflected from tissue; used to image internal organs or structures, e.g., tumor within a gland; may help to determine if a lump is solid tissue or cystic: *also called* **sonography**.

understaging assignment of a lower than actual clinical stage at initial diagnosis because of the difficulty of assessing the available information with accuracy, (e.g., stage T2b as opposed to T3b).

under study being reviewed by a drug firm, university or private laboratory.

unilateral extracapsular extension prostate cancer that has grown through one lobe of the prostate and into the surrounding tissue: *also known as* **locally advanced prostate cancer**.

unit measure of a substance, such as a drug or fluid, (e.g., a pint of blood equals a unit of blood).

United States Pharmacopoeia (USP) sets purity standards for drugs.

University of Texas under review at the University of Texas Center (Houston) for Alternative Medicine (UT-CAM); established by the Office of Alternative Medicine (OAM) as the only OAM-supported institution focused solely on alternative and complementary cancer treatments.

uPA urokinase plasminogen activator substance made by tumor cells to stimulate both tumor and the osteoblast: *see* **ATF**.

Uprima apomorphine (TAP Holdings): impotency pill that claims to achieve erection in 10 to 20 minutes.

ureter anatomical tube that drains urine from the kidneys into the urinary bladder.

urethra tube that drains urine from the urinary bladder; divided into the prostatic urethra and penile urethra.

urethral stricture scarring and narrowing of the urethra; may be a complication of surgery or chronic infection.

urethritis inflammation of the urethra.

urethrorectal fistula closed passage leading from the bladder through the prostate gland and out through the penis; occurs after prolonged urethal and subrapubic catheter drainage.

urge incontinence condition in which abnormal urinary bladder contractions forces urine flow through the urethra.

urgency need to urinate very soon.

uric acid part of the blood-chemistry panel test: constituent in the blood that is associated with purine metabolism, normally excreted in the urine: a high value may indicate gout, arthritis, or certain kidney problems; a low value is not clinically significant.

urinalysis study of the urine; aids in diagnosis of disease states.

urinary imaging studies ultrasound test to look for abnormalities in the bladder.

urinary incontinence inability to prevent the discharge of urine.

urinary retention complete or partial retaining of urine; characterized by the inability to fully empty the urinary bladder: *see* **residual urine**.

urinary system group of organs that permit excess filtered fluids to exit the body.

urinary tract infection (UTI) infection caused by bacteria or other agents, present in the urine; may be associated with fever or with a burning sensation on urination.

urine specimen, 24-hour test in which all of the urine voided in a 24-hour period is collected and tested.

URO urologist.

urodynamic pressure-flow study placement of recording devices into the bladder and rectum to indicate pressure differences generated by bladder muscle contraction.

urodynamic testing examines the function of the bladder and urethral sphincter.

uroflowmetry an electronic recording that measures the speed of the urine flow.

urologic oncologist urologist trained and certified in oncology.

urologist physician who has trained as a surgeon and who has specialized in disorders of the genitourinary system.

urology branch of medicine dealing with disorders of the urinary system in men and women, and the genital organs in men.

Urowave (Dornier Med Tech): brand name microwave thermotherapy device used to treat benign prostatic hyperplasia.

US *see* **ultrasound**.

UTI *see* **urinary tract infection**.

uva-ursi leaf *Uvae ursi folium* herb used for infections of the urinary tract: *see* **German Commission E.**

V

vaccine any preparation of inactivated or killed bacteria or other microorganisms introduced in the body to produce immunity to a specific disease by causing the formation of antibodies.

vacuum-erection device (VED) tube that covers the penis, creates a vacuum, and draws blood into the organ; tube is removed, and a ring placed over the penis to help maintain an erection.

vacuum-tumescent-enhancement therapy mechanical, nonsurgical method of enlarging the penis via a vacuum.

validity extent to which a test actually measures what it claims; used to refer to the effectiveness of therapy.

vascular indicative of a copious blood supply; blood vessels.

vascular infiltration invasion lymphatics or veins, tumor cells indicating distant spread.

vasculitis inflammation of blood vessels.

vas deferens tube through which sperm travels from the testes to the prostate prior to ejaculation.

vasectomy surgery to make a man sterile by cutting the vas deferens, thus preventing passage of sperm from the testes to the seminal vesicles, etc.

Vasomax tretinoin (Schering): drug used for erectile dysfunction as an oral therapeutic agent.

vector virus, or a small piece of DNA, that carries a modified or foreign gene; delivers the desired gene to a target cell; *under study.*

VED *see* **vacuum erection device**.

vegan *see* **ovolactovegetarians**.

VEGF vascular endothelial growth compound, one of 15 proteins known to activate endothelial-cell growth and movement: *see* **endothelial cells, bFGF, EGF**.

VEGF inhibitor (anti-VEGF compound) antiangiogenesis drug in clinical trial; *under study.*

Venlafaxine hydrochloride (Mayo Clinic): antidepressant drug for alleviation of hot flashes in men who are undergoing androgen ablation therapy for prostate cancer; *under study.*

ventral located toward the abdomen.

venus fly trap claimed to be copy of carnivora: *see* **carnivora**.

vesicle small sac containing fluid.

viadur (Alza/Abbott): implant treatment for advanced prostate cancer; *under study.*

Viagra sildenafil (Pfizer): drug used for erectile dysfunction increases blood flow to the penis in response to sexual stimulation; should not be used with any medication that contains nitrates; with the antibiotic erythromycin; with the ulcer drug cimetidine; or by anyone with heart, liver or kidney problems.

Vinblastine with estramustine the two drugs demonstrated anti-mitotic effects in the DU 145 human prostate cancer cell line; *under study.*

Vioxx rofecoxib (Merck): drug used to treat acute pain.

virus microorganism, or a large protein molecule, that cannot be seen with a conventional light microscope; can multiply only within living cells.

vit vitamin.

vitamin compounds which activate enzymes to initiate and control chemical reactions in the body; necessary for virtually all of the biochemical processes of life, such as producing energy, fighting disease, and repairing injured tissues.

vitamin A compound which helps cells reproduce normally, maintain healthy cell membranes; sources are dark green and orange-yellow vegetables, liver, dairy, and cod liver oil.

vitamin B-complex combination of B vitamins; it might be more beneficial to take a B-complex than a single B vitamin.

vitamin B-1 thiamin; compound which helps to process carbohydrates, fat and protein; sources are whole wheat, peas, beans, peanuts, and meat.

Vitamin B-2 riboflavin; compound which helps to process amino acid, fat, and activates folic acid; sources are dairy products, meat, and leafy green vegetables.

vitamin B-3 niacin; compound which helps to regulate cholesterol; sources are peanuts, brewer's yeast, fish, and meat.

Vitamin B-6, B-7 *see* **bioton**.

vitamin B-8 folic acid; compound which may keep homocysteine (an amino acid) levels in blood from increasing; sources are beans, leafy green vegetables, citrus fruits, beets, and wheat germ.

vitamin B-17 trade name for laetrile, a synthetic compound made from amygdalin, a chemical in the kernels of apricot pits, apple seeds, almonds, etc.; promoters use a theory that cancer results from a vitamin deficiency. A 1982 clinical trial sponsored by the National Cancer Institute treated 178 patients with laetrile, and not one was cured, stabilized, or manifested any lessening of cancer-related symptoms.

vitamin C ascorbic acid; found in fruits and vegetables; may have preventive effects against a variety of human cancers: *see* **University of Texas**.

vitamin D colecalciferol; compound which enhances absorption of calcium from food; some studies suggest that vitamin D is an important supplement for men with prostate problems.

vitamin E antioxidant; may enhance the body's immune system which is important in cancer prevention; a trial in Finland with 26,000 men showed that vitamin E reduced prostate cancer deaths by 40 percent. The natural forms, which have a "d" prefix, are preferred, the synthetic forms have a "dl" prefix.

vitamin K-3 and vitamin C (Lake Erie College of Osteopathic Medicine, Erie, PA): combination that appears to destroy prostate cancer cells in mice with tumors composed of human prostate cancer cells; *under study*.

Vitamin M *see* **folic acid**.

vitaxin (Ixsys): antibody that inhibits the process of angiogenesis; *under study*.

VP-16 etoposide (Immunex): generic chemotherapy agent used as an agent in the treatment of refractory testicular tumors.

vuka Zimbabwe's natural remedy, a herb that may enhance male sexual performance.

W

warfarin *see* **Coumadin**.

watchful waiting (WW) observation and monitoring of, or by, a patient without actual treatment.

watchful waiting chemoprevention trial (University of Pennsylvania Cancer Center): for men with a PSA of four or greater and have had a negative biopsy; no indication of cancer; study compares various doses of selenium versus a placebo; *under study*.

water plantain *Alisma plantago-aquatica* herb used to treat diseases of the urinary bladder and urinary tract; poisonous when fresh.

WBC white blood count, part of the complete blood count: white cell (leucocyte) count relates to the body's immune system; colds, allergies, infections, or chemical exposures may cause this value to be high or low.

well differentiated (WD) characteristic of Gleason grades 1 and 2 prostate cancer cells; such tumors are similar to normal prostate cells and tend not to be aggressive.

Whitmore-Jewett staging *see* **staging, tumor or cancer**.

wild-type gene term used to describe the normal nonmutated, nonaltered gene or allele in the genome.

willow herb *Epilobium species* available as a tea or as a vegetable; used for prostate disorders; treatment not proven.

ww *see* **watchful waiting**.

X

X chromosome one of the two chromosomes that determine gender: female cells contain two X chromosomes; male cells contain one X and one Y. A gene called HPCX, located on the X chromosome; may account for 16 percent of inherited prostate cancers.

xenograft model clones of human prostate cancer tumor cell lines.

xenotransplantation use of animal organs for transplant to human beings.

X-ray type of high-energy radiation that can be used at low levels to make images of the internal structures of the body.

XRT *see* **external beam radiation therapy**.

Y

Yohimbine drug found generally ineffective for erectile dysfunction, according to the American Urological Association.

Z

zinc mineral which is found in low concentration in non-cancerous prostates; zinc consumed in supplements may be absorbed into prostate tissue.

Zofran zofran (Glaxo Wellcome): drug used to treat postoperative vomiting and nausea in adults.

Zoladex goserelin acetate (Zeneca/Astra): analog used in the palliative hormonal treatment of advanced prostate cancer; it may sometimes be used as an adjuvant and neoadjuvant hormonal treatment of earlier stages of prostate cancer.

Zoladex and radiation combination therapy approved for treatment of local and advanced prostate cancer in Canada.

Zoledronate (Novartis/CibaGeneva): bisphosphonate compound that may decrease the occurrence of skeletal-related complications of prostate cancer patients; *under study*.

zone part or area of an organ.

zone, prostate term used to describe an anatomic relationship in the prostate; comprised of three anatomical zones; central, peripheral, and transition.

zones prostate has five zones or regions; the urethra is surrounded by the transition zone, which surrounds the central zone; the largest and outer portion is called the peripheral zone; two smaller areas are the periurethral zone which surrounds the upper urethra and the fibromuscular zone, a layer of smooth muscle that runs along the top and sides of the prostate.

Appendix One

Association Abbreviations

AACR American Association for Cancer Research, Inc.

ACAM American College for Advancement in Medicine, Laguna Hills, CA.

ACOR Association of Cancer Online Resources.

ACS American Cancer Society.

AFIP Armed Forces Institute of Pathology.

AFUD American Foundation for Urologic Disease.

AGA American Gastroenterology Association.

AHA American Heart Association.

AHCPR Agency for Health Care Policy and Research.

AICR American Institute for Cancer Research.

ALCASE Alliance for Lung Cancer Advocacy, Support and Education.

AMA American Medical Association.

ANNA Artificial Neural Network Analysis.

ASCO American Society of Clinical Oncology.

ASTRO American Society for Therapeutic Radiology and Oncology.

AUA American Urological Association.

BCBSA Blue Cross and Blue Shield Association.

CALGB The Cancer and Leukemia Group B; a national network of 31 university medical schools and more than 185 community hospitals with more than 3,000 physicians; funded by NCI, involved in prostate cancer clinical trials.

CaP Cure The Association for the Cure of Prostate Cancer.

CARE Cancer Alternatives Research Exchange.

CCC Comprehensive Cancer Centers.

CCSG Cancer center support grants (NCI)

CDER Center for Drug Evaluation and Research (FDA).

CGAP *see* Cancer Genome Anatomy Project (NCI).

CHAMPUS Civilian Health and Medical Program for the Uniformed Services.

Circle Internet support group for significant others of men with PC.

CIS Cancer Information Service (NCI).

CLIA Clinical Laboratory Improvement Act; current law stipulates that only laboratories regulated by the CLIA can generate results for use in patient care.

COPR Council Of Public Representatives (NIH).

CPDR Center for Prostate Disease Research (Department of Defense).

CPMP Committee for Proprietary Medicinal Products (Europe).

CRC Clinical Research Center.

CRI Cancer Research Institute.

DHHS Department of Health and Human Services.

DoD Department of Defense.

DSHEA Dietary Supplement Health and Education Act of 1994; curtailed the FDA's authority over any product labeled "supplement," providing it made no assertion to affect a disease.

EAEMP European Agency for the Evaluation of Medicinal Products.

ECOG Eastern Cooperative Oncology Group.

ECPCP Education Center for Prostate Cancer Patients.

EORTC European Organization for Research and Treatment of Cancer.

EPC Evidence-based Practice Center.

EPIC Empowered Patients in Control, a guide for men with advanced prostate cancer and for their families and health providers.

FASB Federation of American Societies for Experimental Biology.

FDA Food and Drug Administration.

German Commission E The German Regulatory Authority's herbal watchdog agency; considered the world's leading authority on herbal medicines (Germany).

HCFA Health Care Financing Administration of Medicare.

HMO Health Maintenance Organization.

IBIDS International Bibliographic Information on Dietary Supplements NIH).

ICPCG International Consortium for Prostate Cancer Genetics.

IRB Institutional Review Board, health professionals who must approve a clinical study.

LCA Leukemia Society of America.

MSK Memorial Sloan-Kettering, a well-known cancer hospital in New York City.

MTF Military Treatment Facility.

NAFC National Association for Continence.

NBLIC National Black Leadership Initiative on Cancer.

NCCN National Comprehensive Cancer Network.

NCCS National Coalition of Cancer Survivors.

NCI National Cancer Institute.

NHF National Health Federation.

NIA National Institute on Aging.

NIDCR National Institute of Dental and Craniofacial Research.

NIEHS National Institute for Environmental and Health Science (NIH).

NIH National Institutes of Health.

NLM National Library of Medicine (NIH).

NOF National Osteoporosis Foundation.

NPCC The National Prostate Cancer Coalition.

NPCDP National Prostate Cancer Detection Project, ACS; multi-institutional study involving 2,000 men.

NPCP National Prostatic Cancer Project.

OAM Office of Alternative Medicine, under NIH.

OBA Office of Biotechnology Activities (NIH).

ODS Office of Dietary Supplements (NIH).

OPRR Office of Protection from Research Risks, a federal agency.

PAACT Patient Advocates for Advanced Cancer Treatments.

PCAN Prostate Cancer Action Network.

PCC Prostate Cancer Charity (Great Britain).

PCOG Prostate Cancer Oncology Group.

PCOS *see* PCOS Prostate Cancer Outcomes Study (NCI).

PCPT *see* PCPT Prostate Cancer Prevention Trial (NCI).

PCREF Prostate Cancer Research and Education Foundation.

PCRI Prostate Cancer Research Institute.

PDQ Physicians Data Query; an NCI-supported database available to physicians, containing current information on standard treatments and ongoing clinical trials.

PLCO see PLCO Prostate, Lung, Colorectal, and Ovarian Cancer Trial (NCI).

PORT Prostate Disease Outcomes Research Team (AHCPR).

PPO Preferred Provider Organization.

RCOG Radiotherapy Clinics of Georgia.

REAP Research Enhancement Awards Program, a NIH research funding program.

PRG Prostate Cancer Progress Review Group (NCI).

RTOG Radiation Therapy Oncology Group.

SACGT Secretary's Advisory Committee on Genetic Testing (NIH).

SACI San Antonio Cancer Institute.

SBIR Small Business Innovation Research Program, a NIH research funding program.

SEER *see* SEER surveillance, epidemiology and end results (NCI),

SFSA Stay Fine–Stay Alive, slogan of the National Black Leadership Initiative on Cancer.

SPOREs Specialized Programs of Research Excellence (NCI),

STTR Small Business Technology Transfer Research; a NIH technology transfer program between small business firms and nonprofit research institutions.

SUO Society for Urologic Oncology.

UCSF University of California, San Francisco.

USP U.S. Pharmacopoeia, a private non-profit group that sets voluntary standards for drugs, vitamins, and minerals in the U.S.

UT-CAM University of Texas Center for Alternative and Complementary Medicine.

Appendix Two

Guidelines and Questions Regarding Drugs to Ask Your Physician

Keep a current, thorough, and accurate medication and treatment history.

Add new drugs to your written history as soon as you begin taking them.

Note date, when, and reason why a drug is discontinued

Make every visit to your doctor's office a drug consultation; include over-the-counter in addition to prescription medications. If necessary, put them all in a bag and bring to your doctor so he or she can see what others have prescribed.

Write down any questions before going to the doctor.

Ask what each new prescription is for, how to take the drug, and what to do if you miss a dose; should you get up during the night, or is it okay to take it in the morning?

Ask the doctor about potential side effects, and what you should do if they occur.

Ask the doctor what you should do if you get a side effect you weren't told about.

Ask whether the doctor has prescribed this drug for anyone else in your situation. How many?

What were the results?

If the doctor switches you from one drug to another, ask why, especially if the former drug has been successful.

Appendix Three

Professional package labeling commonly known as the "package insert," contains valuable information for you, as a patient.

adverse drug reactions enumeration of adverse reaction to a drug; a requirement of the Food and Drug Administration.

drug abuse adverse reactions as related by the descriptions of susceptible patients.

drug bioassays interval testing of drug concentration in the blood to determine whether the desired therapeutic level is achieved; also used to ascertain toxic levels of a drug when its therapeutic levels are exceeded.

drug contraindications reasons why a drug should not be used because the risk may outweigh any possible benefit; contradictions may be general or specific, (as to age, sex, clinical and medical history), and related to the use of a medication, (over-the–counter or prescription).

drug dependence the potential of a drug to cause dependence and consequent abuse; measured on a five-point scale: schedule I drugs are the most dangerous.

drug indications conditions for which a drug has been approved for treatment.

drug information for patients enumeration and disclosure of the clinical indications of a drug; provided by the physician and pharmacist for the patient before the drug is administered.

drug interactions the known interactions of a drug with other medications.

drug overdose description of the effects of a drug when the prescribed dosage is exceeded.

drug stoppage in general, medications should be used as prescribed, and until exhausted. Failure to complete the full treatment regimen may cause clinical relapse or treatment failure.

drug warnings information regarding the unfavorable side effects of a drug that may result from its use as prescribed.

Drug: How Supplied? When can dosage be adjusted by dividing a tablet?

Medications are supplied in different concentrations. It is often possible to cut a preparation to reduce it to the desired dosage and, at the same time, savon costs; dividing such medication is made relatively easy by using a pill cutter. Check with your pharmacist to determine when pill cutting can be safely and expeditiously carried out.

Appendix Four

Discussion Groups on the Internet

Studies have shown that men who take an active part in learning about their disease have a longer life than those that don't. Click on the site that interests you, and follow their instructions to take part in the subject.

The Circle (Support of the family of men with prostate cancer)
http://www.prostatepointers.org/circle

Hormone Refractory Prostate Cancer
Htto://www.hrpc.org

IceBalls (Cryosurgery for prostate cancer)
http://www.prostatepointers.org/iceballs/

PC SPES (Patients who are interested in *PC SPES* as a treatment for their prostate cancer)
www.pc-spes.com

Prostate Cancer Action Network (Advocacy issues)
http://www.prostatepointers.org/pcan

Prostate Cancer and Intimacy PCAI (Discussions of the sexual issues surrounding PC)
To subscribe, send email to: majordomo@rattler.cameron.edu

Prostate Help Mailing List (PHML)
To subscribe, send email to: listserve@home.ease.1soft.com

Prostate Problems Mailing List
Email to: listserv@listserv.acor.org
Type as message: Sub prostate then your first and last name

Physician to Patient p2p (Information from doctors)
http://prostatepointers.org/p2p

SeedPods (Brachytherapy, or radioactive seed implants)
http://www.prostatepointers.org/seedpods

Virtual Library (A library of documents)
www.prostatepointers.org

Appendix Five

Websites on the Internet

Prostate Cancer Websites

An analysis by *Cyber Dialogue* shows that more than 22 million Americans—36 percent of American web users—used the web to obtain health or medical information (*The Industry Standard,* April 5, 1999, p. 38). Of this group, 46 percent were age 50 and over, and 47 percent were women; fifty-two percent claimed they were investigating diseases. This use of the web is expected to increase to 30 million by 2001.

There are many websites that promote the sale of herbs, drugs, vitamins, etc. These brand-name sites have not been listed.

The sites are broken down by their main thrust. However, most of them have a great deal of additional information.

Note: This listing was current at the time of writing. However, because the Internet is a rapidly changing medium for the exchange of information, some of these addresses may no longer be valid.

* An asterisk indicates a recommended site.

General Prostate Cancer Information

Daily updates on prostate cancer news
http://search.news.yahoo.com/search/news?p=prostate+cancer

* General information about prostate cancer
http://www.pslgroup.com/PROSTCANCER.htm

American Cancer Society
http://www.cancer.org

Ask the cancer specialist
http://www.canceroption.com

Center for Prostate Cancer Disease Research
http://www.cpdr.org

Center Watch; research information
http://www.centerwatch.com/headlines

ECPCP: The Education Center for Prostate Cancer Patients
http://www.ecpcp.org

Feedback help and general information
http://www.lycos.com/health/flash/postatecancer.html

Guide to prostate cancer
http://www.hypertext.org

Hypertext guide to prostate cancer
http://www.hypertext.org

Massachusetts Research Institute
http://www.cure.prostatecancer.com

Patient Advocates for Advanced Prostate Cancer Treatment
http://www.prostatepointer.org/paact

PC dot com
http://www.prostatecancer.com

Personal treatment options
http://www.cancerfacts.com

PPML (Prostate problems mailing list) archives
http://listserv.acor.org/archives/prostate.html

Prostate Cancer Charity—Great Britain
http://www.prostate-cancer.org.uk/about.htm

* Prostate Cancer Information Link
    http://www.comed.com/Prostate

Prostate Cancer News–Albin Foundation
    http://www.achiever.com/freehmpg/mhaythor/mainab.html

Prostate cancer resource guide
    http://www.afud.org/pca/pcaindex.html

* P S A Rising Magazine; up-to-date news
    http://www.psa-rising.com

SciWeb, Resources for Biotechnology Professionals
    http://www.scitalk.com/prostate.cfm

* Search for Valuable Information
    http://www.prostatepointers.org/search_form.html

University of Michigan
    http://www/cancer.med.umich.edu/prostcan/prostcan.html

University of Pennsylvania
    http://oncolink.upenn.edu/disease/prostate

University of Wisconsin Cancer Center
    http://www.medsch.wisc.edu/pca

* Urological Sciences Research Foundation
    http://usrf.org

* Web MD
    http://www.webmd.com

Wellness Web
    http://wellweb.com/

Activists

National Prostate Cancer Coalition
    http://www.4npcc.org

PACNET, a tool box for activists
    http://www.prostatepointers.org/pacnet

Advocates

Patient Advocates
    http://www.patientadvocacy.org

Alternative Treatment

* Center for Alternative Research at University of Texas at Houston
http://www.sph.uth.tmc.edu:8052/utcam

PC Spes; a Chinese herbal combination
http://www.pc-spes.com

Larry Clapp, alternative diets, etc.
http://www.prostate90.com

* Wellness Web for Alternative Medicine
http://www.wellweb.com/AlternativeComplementary_Medicine.htm

Alternative Medicine
http://www.yahoo.com/Health/Alternative_Medicine

Afro-American

Black Health Net
http://www.blackhealthnet.com

Associations

American Society of Clinical Oncology
http://www.asco.org

Uronet for Urologists
http://www.uronet.org

European Association of Urology
http://www.uroweb.org

BPH

Diagnosis and Treatment: US Agency for Health Care and Research
http://www.jr2.ox.ac.uk/Bandolier/band11/b11-3.html

* Prostatitis Foundation
http://www.prostate.org/

Brachytherapy

Seedpods
http://www.prostatepointers.org/seedpods

Clinical Trials, Research, etc.

Definitive source, originated March, 2000
Includes NIH, federal agencies, industry, universities and organizations
http://clinicaltrials.gov/ct/gui/c/b

* CenterWatch Clinical Trials Listing Service
http://www.centerwatch.com

University of Mass.; Research and News
http://members.spree.com/sip/cryosurgery

Dentistry

National Oral Health Information Clearinghouse
http://www.aerie.com/nohicweb

Digest

Organize your clinical information
http://www.prostatepointers.org/rtrax/pcdigest.html

Drugs

* Informative
http://www.dml.georgetown.edu/depts/pharmacology

Hospices

National Hospice Organization
http://www.nho.org

Hospice Hotlinks
http://www.teleport.com/~hospice/links.htm

Humor

HAH, humor about our problems
http://www.prostatepointers.org/mailman/listinfo/hah

Incontinence

Incontinence on the Internet; biofeedback
http://incontinent.com

Impotence

Urological Sciences Research Foundation
http://www.usrf.org

Nutrition

PPML Recipe Book
http://www.prostatepointers.org

Office of Dietary Supplements, NIH
http://odp.od.nih.gov/ods/databases/ibids.html

Pathology

Dr. Jonathan Oppenheimer
http://www.prostatepointers.org/virtual_lab

Patients

National Coalition for Cancer Survivorship
http://www.cansearch.org

* One Man's Opinion
http://prostatelab.com/squarf.htm

* Patients Helping Patients
http://www.cooleyville.com/cancer

Survivors Support group
http://www.heartwarmers4u.com/members/?jimfulks

Watchful Waiting by Tom Feeney
http:www.prostatepointers.org/ww

Virgil's Summary of His Research
http://www.prostate-online.com/

Physicians, Hospitals and Clinics

Dr. Israel Barken
http://www.prostatepointers.org/barken

Dr. Stephen Barrett, Quackwatch
http://www.quackwatch.com

Dr. Nicholas Bruchovsky
http:www.postatepointers.org/

Dr. Fernand Labrie
http:www.prostatepointers.org/labrie

Dr. Robert Leibowitz
http:www.prostatepointers.org/prostate/leibowitz

Dr. Matthew S. Lief
http://www.theurologist.com/prostate_cancer.htm.

Dr. Charles Myers
http:www.prostatepointers.org/cmyers

Dr. Kenneth J. Pienta, University of Michigan
http://www.cancer.med.umich.edu/prostcan/prostcan

Dr. Steve Strum
http://www.prostatepointers.org/strum

M. D. Anderson Cancer Center
http://www.mdanderson.org

Memorial Sloan-Kettering Prostate Cancer Center
http://www.mskcc.org/document/WICPROST.htm

Physicians Talk about Prostate Cancer
http:www.prostatepointers.org/prostate/#talks

Radiation

UNC Chapel Hill Radiosurgery
http://www.med.unc.edu/surgery/radiosurgery

Radiation-Oncology
http:www.radiation-oncology.com

Support Groups

* US TOO International, Inc.
http://www.ustoo.com

Prostate Cancer Search
http://www.medinex.com

Prostate and Cancer and Women
http://www.pcawomen.org

Suburban Boston Men's Health Program
http://www.prostate-ed.org

Government Agencies / Internet Sites

* Practical health care information; Agency for Health Care Policy and Research
http://www.ahcpr.cdc.gov

Centers for Disease Control and Prevention
http://www.cdc.gov

Food and Drug Administration; FDA
http://www.fda.gov

Health and Human Services, loads of links
http://www.healthfinder.com

Health Care Financing Administration; (Medicare/Medicaid information)
http://www.hcfa.gov

National Institutes of Health; NIH
http://www.nih.gov/health

* National Library of Medicine (do a word search on prostate cancer and get 20,000 entries!)
http;//www.ncbi.nlm.nih.gov/PubMed/medline.html

* More Prostate Cancer Links
http://www.cancerlinks.org/prostcanlinks.html

Legal Advice:

Legal Advisory Committee, PAACT
Gregoru H. Teufel
Sweeney, Metz, Fox, McGrann & Schermer
11 Stanwix St. 18th floor
Pittsburgh, PA 15222
email: gteufel@sweeneymetz.com

Publications

Hot Sheet
US TOO International, Inc.
930 N. York Road, Suite 50
Hinsdale, IL 60521

Cancer Communication
PAACT
1143 Parmelee NW
Grand Rapids, MI 49514

PCR Insights
Prostate Cancer Research Institute
5777 Century Blvd. Suite 885
Los Angeles, CA 90045

Prostate Cancer Exchange
The Education Center for Prostate Cancer Patients
380 N. Broadway Suite 304
Jericho, N.Y. 11753

Prostate Forum
Rivanna Health Publications
P.O. Box 6696
Charlottesville, VA 22906

REF Reporter
Prostate Cancer Research & Education Foundation
6699 Alvarado Rd. Ste. 2301
San Diego, CA 92120

Appendix Six

How to Receive Your FREE Personalized MultiGraph

A prostate cancer digest may be submitted for MultiGraph to plot your personal history. Your digest should include the following basic information:

Date

First and last name

Address, ZIP code or Postal code; Country

Day or evening phone numbers; FAX and/or e-mail address

Date of birth

In addition, please include any or all the following available information:

Gleason

Clinical stage

Prostate volume

Ploidy, Partin, Narayan

Diagnosis

The date and level of every PSA blood test ever taken, (in chronological order). Other numerical blood test results may be included for plotting.

The start and stop dates of all treatments, medications, supplements, or life style changes.

Date and result of any diagnostic tests or procedures, such as bone scan, ProstaScint, CT scan, prostatectomy, cryosurgery, etc., or other significant events.

A good approach is to list all dates in chronological sequence, following each date by what happened on that date.

Your digest MUST be sent via e-mail or typewritten so that it can be scanned for optical character recognition. Due to the volume of requests, handwritten digests cannot be accepted.

Send it to: JFistere@email.msn.com

If Internet access is not available, the typed digest can be mailed to: John Fistere, Prostate Cancer Research and Education Foundation, 6699 Alvardo Road, Suite 2301, San Diego, CA 92120 (619) 287-6682.Please include a legal size, stamped, self-addressed envelope.

The Prostate Cancer Research and Education Foundation is a 501(c)(3)not-for-profit organization. Donations are welcome and are tax-deductible.

Appendix Seven

Manufacturers, Distributors, and Research Facilities

Drugs and Products Related to Prostate Cancer

Abbott Laboratories
100 Abbott Park Road
Abbott Park, IL 60064
(800) 255-5162
Actiq, Genset, Heparin, Hytrin, ns-49, sar, Viadur.

Agouron Pharmaceuticals
10350 N.Torrey Pines
La Jolla, CA 92037
(619) 622-3000
AG 3340

A. G. Scientific
450 Lusk Blvd. Suite E 102
San Diego, CA 92121
(877) 452-9925
Suramin

Ajinomoto Co.
15-1 Kyobashi 1-chrome Chuo-ku
Tokyo 104-
Japan 81(3) 5250-8111
Lentinan

Albany College of Medicine
47 New Scotland Ave.
Albany, NY 12208
(518) 262-5521
Marijuana Patch

Alza Pharmaceuticals
950 Page Mill Road
Palo Alto, CA 94303
(800) 227-9953
Ditropan XL, Duros, Elmiron, Testoderm TTS C111, Viadur

American Biologics
Mexico
Bioelectrical therapy, Dioxychlor,HLB. Honvan, LBA

American Medical Systems
10700 Bren Road W.
Minnetonka, MN 55343
(612) 933-4666
Acticon, AMS 700, Sphincter 800

Amgen, Inc.
1840 DeHavilland Dr.
Thousand Oaks, CA 91230-1789
(800) 282-6436
Abarelix, Epogen, Neupogen

Aronex Pharmaceuticals
8707 Tech. Forest Pl.
Woodlands, Texas 77381
(281) 367-1666
Atragen

ArthoCare Corp.
595 N. Pastoria
Sunnyvale, CA 94086
Bipolar urological loop

Astra/Zeneca
50 Otis St.
Westborough, MA 01581
(508) 366-1100
Casodex, Iressa ZD1839, Tamoxifen

Baylor College of Medicine
One Baylor Road
Houston, Texas 77030
(713) 798-4712
Acyclovir, caveolin

Berlex Laboratories, Inc.
300 Fairfield Ave.
Wayne, NJ 07470
(201) 694-4100
Climara

Beth Israel Deaconess Medical
330 Brookline
Boston, MA. 02215
(617) 667-7000
Canstatin

Boehringer Ingelheim Phar., Inc.
900 Ridgebury Road
Ridgefield, CT 06877
(203) 798-9988
Flomax

Botanic Labs
2900-B Saturn St.
Brea, CA 92821
(800) 242-5555
PC SPES

Bristol-Myers Squibb
Box 5254
Princeton, N J 08543
(800) 422-8811
BMS-217380, Chirosciene, Megace, Paclitaxel, Taxol

British Biotech
Annapolis, MD
(800) 355-6957
Marimastat

Calydon, Inc.
1324 Shakespeare Terrace
Sunnyvale, CA (408) 734-0733
CN 706, CV 787

Cell Pathways
702 Electronic Dr.
Horsham, PA 19044
(215) 706-3800
Aptosyn, Exisulind

Ciba Geneva Corp.
556 Morris Ave.
Summit, NJ 07901
(800) 742-2422
Zoledronate

Ciphergen Biosystems
490 San Antonio Road
Palo Alto, CA 94306
(650) 496-3770
Proteinchip

Cochrane, Jack
3769 Bridle Pass
Ann Arbor, MI 48104
Csingle@juno.com
Squeezer

Cytogen Corp.
600 College Road E.
CN 5308, Princeton, N J 08540
(609) 520-3082
CYT 356, Quadramet

Cytran, Inc.
Kirkland, WA
(425) 889-5808
IM 862

Dana Farber Cancer Institute
44 Binney St.
Boston, MA
(617) 632-5100
Beta-lapachone

DuPont Merck Pharma. Co.
331 Treble Cove Rd
N. Billerica, MA 01862
(800) 635-2683
Coumadin, Pyridium, Revia, Surlyn

EDAP TechNomed, Inc.
100 Pinnacle Way, Suite 100
Norcross, GA 30071
(770) 446-9950
Ablatherm, HIFU, Prostatron

Endorex Corp.
900 North Shore Dr.
Lake Bluff, IL 60044
(847) 604-7555
ImmTher

EntreMed Rockville, MD
See **University of Wisconsin**
2-methoxyestradiol, Angiostatin, Endostatin

Forest Pharmaceuticals
909 3rd Ave., 23rd floor
New York, NY 10022
(314) 344-8870
Monural

Genentech, Inc.
460 Point San Bruno Dr.
South San Francisco, CA 94080
(415) 225-1000
Anti-VEGF, Herceptin

Genzyme General
One Kendall Square
Cambridge, MA 02139
(617) 252-7500
Angiogenesis inhibitor, AT III

Glaxo Wellcome
5 Moore Drive
Research Triangle Park, NC 27709
(800) 722-9292
Zofran

Harvard Medical School
25 Shattuck St.
Boston, MA 02115
(617) 432-1000
Htert

Hoechst Marion Roussel, Inc.
10236 Marion Pk. Dr.
Kansas City, MO 64134
(800) 552-3656
Actonel, Anandron, Anzemet, Ditropan XL, Nilandron, Suprefact

Hoffman LaRoche
CH-4070
Basel, Switzerland
(41) 61 688-1111
DeCode genetics

Introgen Therapeutics, Inc.
301 Congress Ave.
Austin, TX 78701
Adenoviral - p53

John Hopkins Medical Institutions
720 Rutland Ave.
Baltimore, MD 21205
(410) 955-5000
ABT-627, alcohol-absolute, artificial neural network, bioimpedance, gene therapy vaccine, mu opiate

Human Genome Sciences
9410 Key West Ave.
Rockville, MD 20850
(301) 309-8504
meth-1, meth-2

Idun Pharmaceuticals, Inc.
11085 N. Torrey Pines Rd.
La Jolla, CA 92037
Sar

Imagyn Medical Technologies
5 Civic Plaza
Newport Beach, CA 92660
(888) 876-4584
Esteem

ImClone Systems, Inc.
180 Varick St.
New York, NY
(212) 645-1405
C 225, IMC-1C11

Immunex/Lederle Labs.
51 University St.
Seattle, WA 98101
(800) 466-8639
Novantrone, VP-16

Implant Sciences
107 Audubon Road # 5
Wakefield, MA 01880
(781) 246-0700
I-plant

Indigo/Johnson & Johnson
Camp Hill Road
Ft. Washington, PA 19034
(215) 233-7000
Genset, Palladium 103, procrit, Thera Seed

IXSYS, Inc.
3550 General Atomics Court
San Diego, CA 92121
(619) 597-4990
Vitaxin

Janssen Pharmaceuticals
1125 Trenton-Harbourton Rd.
Titusville, N J 08560
(800) 544-2987
Liazal, Nizoral

Johnson & Johnson
See **Indigo/Johnson & Johnson**

Ligand Pharmaceuticals
10275 Science Center Dr.
San Diego, CA 92121
(858) 550-7500
altretinoin

Lilly, Eli, & Co.
Lilly Corporate Center
Indianapolis, IN 46285
(800) 545-5979
Evista

MacroChem Corp.
110 Hartwell Ave.
Lexington, MA 02173
(781) 862-4003
SEPA, Topiglan

Mannatech, Inc.
600 S. Royal Lane, Ste. 200
Coppell, TX 75019
(972) 471-7400
Ambrotose

Matritech
330 Nevada St.
Newton, MA 02160
(617) 928-0820
NMP 22 test kit

Mayo Clinic
200 First St., SW
Rochester, MN 55905
(507) 266-5800
ExMI, FISH, Venlafaxine hydrochloride

Maxim Pharmaceuticals
8899 University Center Lane
San Diego, CA
(619) 453-4040
Maxamine

Medarex, Inc.
1545 Route 22E
Annandale, NJ 08801
(908) 713-6001
MDX-210

Medtronic
800 53 Ave., NE
Minneapolis, MN 55421
(800) 328-0810
Interstim continence control therapy

Memorial Sloan Kettering Cancer Center
New York, NY
(800) 525-2225
Id1, Id3, Neurons-spinal cord, Oltipraz, polyvalent antibody inducing vaccine, Pten, Saha, Soy, tf, tn

Merck & Co.
P. O. Box 4
West Point, PA 19486
(800) 672-6372
C 225, Decadron, Finasteride, Fosamax, Proscar, Vioxx

Merz Pharmaceuticals
P.O. Box 18806
Greensboro, NC 27419
(800) 334-0514
Prednisone

Monash Institute
246 Clayton Road
Clayton 3168
Victoria, Australia
(61) 3 9550 5523
Nv-06

National Institute of Dental & Craniofacial Research
45 Center Dr.
Bethesda, MD 20892
Osteonectin

NeoPharm, Inc.
100 Corporate N. Suite 215
Bannockburn, IL 60065
(847) 295-8678
LED, LEP

Nutraceutical Corp.
1400 Kearns Blvd.
Park City, Utah 84060
Permixon

New York Methodist Hospital
506 6th St.
Brooklyn, NY
(718) 780-3000
Testicle transplant

New York Presbyterian Hospital
622 West 168 St.
New York, NY 10032
(212) 305-2500
Atragen

Nexmed
350 Corporate Blvd.
Robbinsville, NJ 08691
(609) 208-9688
Alprostadil

North American Scientific, Inc.

Chatsworth, CA.
Apomate, Iodine-125, Palladium-103

Northwestern Medical School
633 Clark St.
Evanston, IL 60208
(312) 503-8649
Topiglan

Novartis Corp.
564 Morris Ave.
Summit, N. J. 07901
(908) 522-6752
Aredia, ISIS 3521, Sandostatin, Zoledronate

Nycomed Amersham Imaging
2636 S. Clearbrook Dr.
Arlington Heights., IL 60005
(800) 228-0126
Metastron, Oncoseed

Ortho-McNeil Pharmaceuticals
Route 2, P. O. Box 300
Raritan, NJ 08869
(800) 682-6532
Ultram

Oxigene, Inc.
Drug Development
Boston, MA
(617) 536- 9500
Combretastatin A4

Perdue Pharma L. P.
100 Connecticut Ave.
Norwalk, CT 06856
(203) 853-0123
Oxycontin

Pfizer
235 East 42 St.
New York, NY 10015
(800) 532-4440
Cardura, Viagra

Pharma Mar, S.A.
320 Putman Ave.
Cambridge, MA 02139
(617) 868-3797
Aplidine, Kahalide F

Pharmacia & Upjohn
P. O. Box 22969
Rochester, NY 14692
(800) 727-8984
Acylfulvenes, Adriamycin, Caverject, Depot-Provera, Detrol, Dostinex, Emcyt, Linomide, MGI 114

Proteo Protein Sciences
1000 Research Pkwy.
Meriden, CT 06450
PY1-00703

Procter & Gamble Pharmaceuticals
11450 Grooms Rd
Cincinnati, OH 45242
(800) 448-4878
Actonel, Didronel

Quest Diagnostics
One Malcolm Ave.
Teterboro, NJ 07608
(800) 631-1390
Chemiluminescent assays

Rhone-Poulenc Rorer
500 Arcola Road
Collegeville, PA 19426
(610) 454-8000
Taxotere

Rice University
6100 Main St.
Houston, TX 77005
(713) 348-0000
Nanotechnology

Roche Pharmaceuticals
340 Kingsland St.
Nutley, NJ 07110
(800) 526-6367
Ibandronate, Rocaltrol

SafeScience
31 St. James Ave., Suite 520
Boston, MA 02116
(800) 260-6843
GBC-590

Sandoz Pharmaceutical Co.
Route 10
East Hanover, NJ 07936
(800) 503-6673
Miacalcin

Schering Corp.
200 Galloping Hill Rd.
Kenilworth, NJ 07033
(800) 222-7579
Androcur, Eulexin, Depot-Provera, Vasomax

Schwartz Pharma, Inc.
P.O.Box 2038
Milwaukee, WI 53201
(800) 558-5114
Edex

Searle/Pfizer
P. O. Box 5110
Chicago, IL 60680
(800) 323-1603
Celebrex

Sigma Pharmaceuticals
(Sigma-Aldrich)
Lexington, KY.
TGF-B

SmithKline Beecham
P.O. Box 1467
Pittsburgh, PA 15230
(800) beecham
Kytril, Progenitor

Solvay Pharmaceuticals
901 Sawyer Road
Marietta, GA 30062
(770) 578-9000
Estratab, Prometrium

Sonus Pharmaceuticals, Inc.
22026 20th Ave., Ste. 102
Bothell, WA 98021
(425) 487-9500
EchoGen 851

Sugen (Pharmacia & Upjohn)
South San Francisco, CA
(800) SUGEN-06
RL 0903, SU 101, SU 5416, SU 6668

Synsorb Biotech, Inc.
(403) 283-5900
Reolyson

TAP Holdings/Pharmaceuticals
2355 Waukegan Road
Deerfield, IL 60015
(800) 622-2011
Apomorphine SL, Lupron, tnp-470, Uprima

Theragenics Corp.
5325 Oakbrook Pkwy.
Norcross, GA 30093
(800) 458-4372
Palladium 103

Thesus Imaging
see **North American Scientific**

Tosoh Medics, Inc.
373 Vintage Park Drive
Foster City, CA 94404
(800) 248-6764
PSA tests

Trimedyne, Inc.
2801 Barranca Road
Irvine, CA 92606
(949) 559-5300
nd: yag

University of Calgary
2500 University Drive
Calgary, Alberta
T2N IN4 Canada
(403) 220-5110
Reovirus

University of Illinois-Chicago
Box 5220
Chicago, IL 60680
(312) 996-7000
Pifithrin-alpha (PFTa)

University of Michigan
20 S. University Ave.
Ann Arbor, MI 48109
(734) 764-9356
PHSRN, Tetrathiomolyboat

University of Nebraska
501 N. 14 St.
Lincoln, NE 68588
(402) 472-7211
15 KD

University of Texas-Houston
School of Public Health
Center for Complementary and Alternative Medicine Research
7000 Fannin St.
Houston, Texas 77030
(713) 792-5909

University of Wisconsin-Madison
716 Langdon St.
Madison, WI 53706
(608) 262-1234
Angiostatin, Endostatin, E vitamin,2-methoxyestradiol

UroCor, Inc.
800 Research Parkway
Oklahoma City, OK 73104
(800) 634-9330
Quantitative nuclear grade

Urologix, Inc.
14405 21st Ave.
N. Plymouth, MN 55447
(612) 475-1400
Targis d4 system

UroMed Corp.
64 A Street
Needham, MA 02194
(617) 433-0033
CaverMap Surgical Aid

Vertex Pharmaceuticals, Inc.
130 Waverly St.
Cambridge, MA 02139
(617) 577-6000
Incel

Vical, Inc.
9373 Towne Centre Dr., Suite 100
San Diego, CA 92121
(858) 646-1100
Leuvectin

VidaMed
6107 Landing Parkway
Freemont, CA 94538
(800) 328-8781
TUNA

Vion Pharmaceuticals, Inc.
4 Science Park
New Haven, CT. 06511
(203) 498-4210
Tapet

Vivus, Inc.
545 Middlefield Road.
Menlo Park, CA 94025
(800) 367-6873
Muse

Yeshiva University Einstein College
1300 Morris Park Ave.
Bronx, N.Y. 10461
(877) 444-5250
CLAL

Wyeth-Ayerst
P.O. 8299
Philadelphia, PA 19101
CAP-676. PremPro

Zeneca/Astra
1800 Concord Pike
P. O. Box 15437
Wilmington, DE 19850
(800) 424-3727
Casodex, IRESSA ZD 1839, Tamoxifen, Zoladex